THE WELSH BOY

Julian Mitchell

THE WELSH BOY

adapted from
The True Anti-Pamela by James Parry

OBERON BOOKS
LONDON

WWW.OBERONBOOKS.COM

First published in 2012 by Oberon Books Ltd
521 Caledonian Road, London N7 9RH
Tel: +44 (0) 20 7607 3637 / Fax: +44 (0) 20 7607 3629
e-mail: info@oberonbooks.com
www.oberonbooks.com

A catalogue record for this book is available from the British Library.

PB ISBN: 978-1-84943-455-3
E ISBN: 978-1-84943-607-6

Cover image 'Miss O'Murphy', by Francois Boucher

INTRODUCTION

On Sunday 22 February 1736 there was a fracas at Great House, Llantilio Crossenny, eight miles west of Monmouth, halfway along the road to Abergavenny. James Parry, a 'mad and drunk' young Welsh music master and organist, was trying to force his way in to see Mary Powell, the mistress who had recently been prevented by her furious mother from seeing him. Mary and her mother, forewarned, were in the parlour, protected by armed servants who threw him out. He retired to the pub at the house's gates, drank still more, then fell asleep. He was woken to be arrested by the local constable, then fell asleep again. In the morning he remembered nothing of what had happened. Great House, though, did remember, and it pursued him relentlessly through the courts for the next year. Parry came from Carmarthen where his father was a hair merchant; Mary Powell was of an old gentry family, connected to many of the 'best people' in Monmouthshire and Herefordshire, and she was worth five or six thousand pounds, a substantial sum. He had, in her vengeful mother's eyes, committed the unforgivable offence of trying to better himself by marrying across the boundary between the classes.

Parry was born in 1712 and as a boy had had a very beautiful treble voice, which won him a place in the cathedral choir in Bristol. Known as 'The Welsh Boy', he was much in demand at concerts there and in Bath. But his adulterous master treated him badly – resentment seems to have been an indelible part of his character from an early age. With the help of his first girl-friend, the daughter of a plantation owner, he ran away to Carolina. But none of his adventures ever ended well, and he was arrested and brought home again, his voice breaking as he came up the Bristol Channel. This early disappointment, though, was nothing compared to the ending of his affair with Mary Powell, and bitter at being jilted of both girl and money, he took his revenge by publishing his memoir of it in July 1741. He called it *The True Anti-Pamela or Memoirs of Mr. JAMES PARRY, late Organist of Ross in Herefordshire. In which are inserted his Amours*

with the celebrated Miss ____ , of Monmouthshire. Written by Himself.
It gives a very circumstantial account of his whole relationship
with Mary, and adds their love-letters for extra scandal. He also
told anecdotes, many discreditable, about several of her extensive
local cousinage, some named and some thinly veiled by the
use of initials. The picture he painted of the Herefordshire and
Monmouthshire gentry in 'the age of elegance' is not elegant at
all. But whatever one may think of his behaviour, the story is a
fascinating and highly dramatic version of the enduring British
obsession with class.

His title needs some explanation. *Pamela, or, Virtue Rewarded,*
by Samuel Richardson was published in 1740 and at once became
the sensational novel of its day, provoking several satirical
parodies; one by Henry Fielding, was called *Shamela*, another, by
Eliza Haywood, *The Anti-Pamela.* Richardson's Pamela is a lower-
class girl, pursued by an upper-class would-be seducer, who is so
overcome by her virtuous resistance that he gives in and marries
her. Parry claimed his memoir told an exact reverse story, true
not fictitious, with himself as an innocent youth offered marriage
by an upper-class young woman who then jilted him. The truth
was proved by the love-letters – the publication of which was also
proof that he was by no means a gentleman. But scandal always
sells, as today's gossip magazines and websites demonstrate day
after day, and the book was an immediate success. Reprinted
within two months, it was honoured, if that's the word, with a
pirated edition the same year. The story continued to find new
readers as late as 1770 when there were two further editions.

Such success might have made Parry happy; but he was no
longer there to enjoy it. After leaving Monmouthshire, he had
various jobs in the musical theatre in London, and one or two
fights in the streets, before, in May 1741, he became Master at
Arms on the *Revenge*, a privateer cruising against the Spanish,
with whom Britain was then at war. Drunk one day in harbour,
he tried to shoot the ship's trumpeter for disobeying his orders.
It is from the trumpeters's account of the *Revenge*'s calamitous
expedition that we learn that on September 10 1741, in a bungled
raid on Tenerife, Parry was himself shot through the heart and
dropped dead. He was buried at sea, probably not even knowing

the second edition of his memoir was about to appear.

Mary Powell, meanwhile, no doubt with her merciless mother's approval, married a lawyer who had taken part in Parry's legal persecution. Like him, John Lewis came from Carmarthenshire, but he had two estates and Parry none. Though a JP for Monmouthshire, he was High Sheriff in Carmarthen in 1749, so perhaps the Lewises kept away from Monmouthshire till the scandal had died down. They had four children. After Mary's death in 1760, John Lewis pulled down Great House and built a rather dull Georgian one in its place, known at Llantilio Court. This, in its turn, was pulled down in 1922, long after the Powell family had died out. Only a few lumps of masonry and some specimen trees still survive there. But neither James Parry nor Mary Powell will be forgotten, so long as nosey readers continue to rediscover Parry's memoir, with its caddish but fascinating account of life in a small town on the Welsh Borders in the 1730s, where dullness was enlivened only by malicious gossip, marital calculation, drink and furtive sex.

Julian Mitchell, 2012

Characters

JAMES PARRY

MARY POWELL

ELIZABETH POWELL

DOOMSDAY/MATTHEW POWELL/DICKY
JEFFRIES/DAVIES/AMBROSE/SEYS

MRS JEFFRIES/BETTY FISHER/DOLLY DEW

The play is set in Ross, Herefordshire, and Llantilio
Crossenny, Monmouthshire.

The time is the 1730s; and now.

The Welsh Boy was commissioned by Theatre Royal Bath, and was first performed in the Ustinov Studio, Theatre Royal Bath on 13 September 2012 with the following cast:

JAMES PARRY	Sion Daniel Young
MARY POWELL	Peta Cornish
ELIZABETH POWELL	Geraldine Alexander
DOOMSDAY/MATTHEW POWELL/ DICKY JEFFRIES/AMBROSE/SEYS	Ed Birch
MRS JEFFRIES/BETTY FISHER/ DOLLY DEW	Rhiannon Oliver

Director Matthew Lloyd
Set and Costume Designer Ti Green
Associate Costume Designer Katie Lias
Lighting Designer Ben Ormerod
Composer and Sound Designer Jon Nicholls

ACT ONE

As the lights go up, we find JAMES PARRY admiring an 18th-century book, stroking the cover, flipping a few pages. He looks up at the audience.

PARRY: Wonderful thing, a book. Not the ink and paper or the leather binding, but the way it holds the essence of the writer and his times, keeps him and them as fresh as the day he wrote it. Doesn't matter what's in it – poems, stories – truth or lies – if you've written a book, you can thumb your nose at death. Here we are, almost three hundred years later, and I'm as alive as I ever was. You may like me, you may not. But I survive. What's the good of that, you'll say. What use is a thumbed nose to my poor drowned bones? Revenge! That's what. The revenge I have, and go on having, on all the bastards who wanted to wipe me out of existence, so they could go on living their mean, strutting, money-grubbing, little lives, without me there to remind them just how mean and money-grubbing and sourly little they were. *(Bitter.)* I loved that beautiful girl. Heart and soul. And when I held her in my arms, she loved me as I loved her, and – *(Beat, then he taps the book.)* This memoir of mine, you know, it sold pretty well. Was reprinted. Several times. And it's true, all true. And for all their fine airs then, those petty gentry, they wrote no books, so they can't defend themselves or answer back. They live now only in my version of them. Their meanness, their heartlessness, their spite and stupidity, their jealousy, are recorded for ever. Or near enough. *(Doubt, then laugh.)* But then so are mine. Revenge is always said to be sweet. But – I don't know. What do you think ?

He goes as the lights change, and music begins on a wheezy organ, suggesting provincial life. It is the 1730s, and we are in the Prospect at Ross, a place where the townspeople promenade below the church. Two young women are coming on: MARY POWELL, a Monmouthshire heiress of 19, and BETTY FISHER, a local milliner. MARY speaks in an educated voice, BETTY in the local accent.

MARY: He's really good-looking.

BETTY: Much better than poor old Mr Apperley! With his nose like an organ-pipe!

MARY: I hope it was only his nose! Or how would Mrs Apperley have managed?

They both giggle. The music splutters, then stops.

BETTY: That old organ! The parish should get him a new one.

MARY: A new organ for the new organist? But what about the one he's brought with him?

More giggles.

BETTY: He looks manly enough to me.

MARY: But people in Hereford say –

BETTY: People in Hereford will say anything.

MARY: But when he sings, his voice is so high. They say it's more like a boy's voice.

BETTY: Perhaps he's a unicorn?

MARY: Not a unicorn, Betty, a – Oh, here he comes. Being condescended to by Doomsday.

John Roberts, an Oxford student known locally as DOOMSDAY, comes on with PARRY. The girls pretend to look at the view, but their attention is really all for PARRY.

DOOMSDAY: No, the Ross organ would be no good for sounding the Last Trump. Very inferior to the one in St Mary's. That has the best organ outside London.

PARRY: One of the best, certainly.

DOOMSDAY: No, the best. Once you've heard it –

PARRY: I have heard it. I've played on it.

DOOMSDAY: Really?

PARRY: I have friends at Oxford.

DOOMSDAY: *(Patronising.)* At Jesus, I suppose? The Welsh college.

PARRY: *(Aggressive.)* Its scholars are as learned as those of any other college, they tell me.

DOOMSDAY: They like to think so, no doubt. But they have a long way to go to catch up. Jesus is such a recent addition to the university.

PARRY: It's been there a hundred and fifty years.

DOOMSDAY: My dear fellow! Balliol was founded in 1263. And it's been the great centre for medical education ever since.

PARRY: It likes to think so, no doubt. *(Quick, before he can reply.)* But why are you doing Medicine? Your father's an attorney, isn't he?

DOOMSDAY: He is.

PARRY: Doesn't he want you to follow him in the law?

DOOMSDAY: He did. But when I explained to him that the world as we know it is nearing its end –

PARRY: Is it?

DOOMSDAY: It says so in Revelations…if you know how to read them. There will be wars, famines, earthquakes, fire – and pestilence and plague. Doctors will be in very great demand. Balliol doctors especially.

PARRY: *(Looking at the view.)* With the river making that great loop down there, the bridge and castle, the church spires, the fields, the woods, the distant mountains – Herefordshire seems more like Arcadia than a place for plague and pestilence.

DOOMSDAY: If you think Ross is Arcadia – *(Laugh.)* It's the most boring town in England. Nothing but innkeepers and fishermen. And all the girls are dressmakers.

PARRY: Women must dress, I suppose.

DOOMSDAY: *(Looking over at MARY POWELL.)* Miss Powell dresses exceptionally well, don't you think?

PARRY: *(Interested.)* Oh, is that Miss Powell?

DOOMSDAY: Wonderful figure. Beautiful complexion. *(Looking down at the river and bridge.)* Ah, here comes the coach to take me back to civilisation. You'll find little enough here, I'm afraid. Unless you can liven the scene yourself. *(Patronising again.)* But next time you're in Oxford, you let me know. I'll show you Balliol chapel, and you can pedal away on our organ to your heart's content.

PARRY: Very kind.

DOOMSDAY: My pleasure!

DOOMSDAY goes over to the girls and doffs his hat. BETTY bobs, but he ignores her completely.

Miss Powell!

MARY: Good morning. Off for the Easter term?

DOOMSDAY: Hilary. At Oxford we call it the Hilary term.

MARY: We shall miss you. Our only man of real learning.

DOOMSDAY: *(Delighted.)* Well! Well! I suppose I am!

MARY: Apart from the rector, of course.

DOOMSDAY: Oh, the rector! *(Patronising laugh.)* He was at Cambridge! Good morning to you!

MARY: Good morning.

He goes.

PARRY: *(To audience.)* His name's Roberts, but everyone calls him Doomsday. He's a conceited fool, whose head has been turned by the metaphysical quacks of Oxford.

He looks again at the view. MARY nudges BETTY.

MARY: Now.

BETTY: No.

MARY: Go on! We must find out what sort of a man he is. If man at all.

BETTY: Then go yourself!

MARY: I can't approach a stranger. Whatever would he think? Go on!

She gives her a push. BETTY goes over to PARRY.

BETTY: Excuse me, Mr Parry –

PARRY: *(Smile.)* I've only been here two days and you know who I am already?

BETTY: Oh, yes, sir.

PARRY: But I don't know you.

BETTY: *(Blush, low.)* Betty Fisher, at your service.

PARRY: What sort of service did you have in mind, Betty?

BETTY: *(Giggle, then loud.)* Miss Powell would like to congratulate you on your appointment, sir.

PARRY: *(Smiling over at MARY.)* Could Miss Powell not congratulate me in person?

BETTY: Oh, no, sir. She's very reserved. *(Whisper.)* Got her position to think of.

PARRY: Has she!

BETTY: *(Posh.)* Says she would not wish to intrude on your – your private reflections.

PARRY: I have all the time in the world for a Miss Powell with a position.

They cross to MARY and he bows. BETTY listens.

Miss Powell? I'm delighted to make your acquaintance.

MARY: *(The grand lady.)* Were you gazing on your birthplace, sir? You are, I believe, from West Wales?

PARRY: Carmarthenshire, yes. But the nearer prospect is far more charming.

MARY: Oh, is it gallantry already?

PARRY: One should always start as one means to go on, surely?

MARY: *(Laugh.)* My mother and I are delighted Ross is to have an organist again. Particularly if he's a merry one. We live close to the church, you see. We like to hear the music.

PARRY: Then I shall play especially for you.

She acknowledges this with a brief social smile, then gets down to what she really wants to know.

MARY: My friends in Hereford say you sing as well as play. That you have an unusually fine voice.

PARRY: Your friends are very kind.

MARY: Very high.

PARRY: It is high, yes.

MARY: And you sing under an Italian name.

PARRY: Signor Perini, yes. Ignorant people think only Italians know how to sing. And I must make a living. So –

MARY: Italians have a – a particular style, don't they?

He realises exactly what she wants to know and decides to tease her. He sings a snatch of song in a very pure falsetto, then smiles at her.

PARRY: Like that?

MARY and BETTY exchange a dubious look.

MARY: To have a voice as high and pure as that, I suppose you had Italian training?

PARRY: Indeed.

MARY: *(Not knowing how to put it.)* One hears that it – the training, that is – the Italian method of training – involves great sacrifices.

PARRY: Great art is not made without them.

MARY: But these sacrifices –

PARRY: The best trained singers earn enormous sums. And money always has its compensations.

MARY: And you – did you make a great sacrifice to obtain your beautiful voice?

PARRY: *(Laugh.)* No, miss. I am as sound as ever I was born. Or I'd now be living in a palazzo in Rome, with my own carriage and servants in livery, not lodged with a widow in Ross and playing a wheezing old organ for a very modest salary.

MARY: *(Pleased.)* I'm sorry about the salary. But since it is so modest, I suppose you will be teaching here as well as playing?

PARRY: Singing, the spinet, the harpsichord, the violin – I shall teach them all.

MARY: Then you must teach me. I need instruction in both singing and the spinet.

PARRY: It will be an honour to attend you.

MARY: I also play the flute.

PARRY: An immoral instrument.

MARY: *(Very surprised.)* Immoral?

PARRY: According to Plato. He thought it incited its audience to wantonness.

BETTY giggles.

It's nonsense, of course. It's a very beautiful instrument, very expressive. Perhaps we could come to an arrangement whereby I teach you the spinet, and you instruct me how to play the flute?

MARY: *(Amused.)* Oh, I'm hardly a proficient.

PARRY: But I should enjoy guidance from your hand. Or lip, I should say. *(She laughs. BETTY giggles again.)* When can our mutual instruction begin?

MARY: Oh, I'm afraid – You will have to talk to Mama.

PARRY gives her a bow. As he comes forward to speak to the audience, the girls go off.

PARRY: Of course I'd never been to Italy in my life. But it was a promising beginning, no? Such a lovely face, such an elegant figure – and such boldness with them! It was almost an invitation to prove my manliness there and then! Yes, she definitely began it, but desire was always there in both of us. Isn't desire the foundation of all love? Without it love is simply affection, surely? And – *(Reads from book.)* I loved Mary Powell as my own soul, and in return she loved me and gave me an infinite deal of pleasure before the affliction which followed. *(Smile at the memory.)* An infinite deal. And I truly loved her, I adored her, though she played me many tricks. Her mother I did not adore. But I soon realised I would have to win her over if I was ever to advance beyond affection with her daughter. So –

ELIZABETH POWELL, 40s, has come on and seated herself in a chair. Though she gives herself grand airs, she smokes a clay pipe, and her clothes are stained with tobacco. PARRY goes and stands before her and she scrutinises him a long moment, puffing.

ELIZABETH: You seem too young to be in charge of sacred music. A mere boy.

PARRY: I'm almost eighteen, madam. And I've been in church choirs since I was ten.

ELIZABETH: Oh, well, in Carmarthen!

PARRY: It is where the Bishop of St David's has his residence. I taught his daughters.

ELIZABETH: To do what?

PARRY: To sing psalms. It was a religious household, of course.

ELIZABETH: Good. Good. Why did you not stay there?

PARRY: Because my voice – I do not care to boast – but my voice gained me a reputation beyond Carmarthen, and when I was twelve, I was sought for to go and sing in Bristol cathedral.

ELIZABETH: Hm. Your mother went with you, I suppose?

PARRY: My mother – *(Deliberate pathos.)* My mother died when I was very young.

ELIZABETH: *(Softened.)* Oh. But you have happy memories of her?

He shakes his head as though too upset to answer.

None at all?

Again he seems unable to speak.

You poor child. But your father – ?

PARRY: My father was always much preoccupied with his business. He was a merchant.

ELIZABETH: What sort of merchant?

PARRY: Hair. He bought and sold hair.

ELIZABETH unconsciously pats her wig.

I was brought up by my sisters.

ELIZABETH: So one of them came to Bristol with you?

PARRY: *(Apparently hesitant.)* Carmarthen – people in Carmarthen are very trusting. And I was trusted, alas, to my mother's cousin Lewis, a watchmaker. It was he arranged my apprenticeship with his friend Mr Priest.

ELIZABETH: *(Confused.)* With a priest?

PARRY: Mr Priest. The cathedral organist. *(Pride.)* My salary was twice as much as any boy before me.

ELIZABETH: *(Severe at once.)* You must not expect riches here in Ross.

PARRY: I did not get them in Bristol, madam. Mr Priest took everything. Priest he may have been by name, but he was a devil to me. *(Pretended shame.)* He took advantage of my innocence.

ELIZABETH: *(Shocked, misunderstanding.)* No!

PARRY nods, eyes down, playing on her suspicions.

But – but –

PARRY: I was so young and – *(Deciding enough was enough.)* He not only received my salary from the dean and chapter, but a fee whenever I sang at concerts.

ELIZABETH: *(Relieved.)* Oh, I thought you meant –

MARY comes to join them.

Mary – Mr Parry is telling me about his master in Bristol.

MARY: *(Sitting.)* Oh?

PARRY: I was in demand at Bath as well as Bristol, you see, miss. The Welsh Boy, they called me. Sometimes, the famous Welsh Boy. People of quality asked for me specially. *(To audience.)* They said I broke hearts with my high notes.

A treble voice sings a brief snatch of Bach's 'Bist Du Bei Mir'.

(To ELIZABETH and MARY.) But when they gave me money privately, after a concert, my master took it from me. He searched my pockets for every last sixpence.

ELIZABETH: I suppose he was entitled to do that. You lived in his house, I assume, you ate at his table? He had a wife?

PARRY: *(Low.)* Yes and no.

ELIZABETH: What do you mean?

PARRY: *(Lowering his voice still more.)* His wife had left him. He was living with another woman.

ELIZABETH: *(Shocked.)* Did the bishop know that?

PARRY: It was hardly a secret in the close.

ELIZABETH: Shocking!

PARRY: She had a son who was also in the choir. *(Contempt.)* His voice was nothing like as good as mine, I could earn twenty shillings where he earned one. So she hated me worse than a quaker does a parrot.

ELIZABETH: *(Frown.)* Than what?

MARY: It's an expression of Mr Congreve's, Mama. From *The Way of the World.*

ELIZABETH has not heard of it.

PARRY: You know it, Miss?

MARY: Oh, yes. There's nothing to do in Ross but read, and I specially like plays. *The Way of the World* is one of my favourites.

ELIZABETH: But quakers? Parrots?

PARRY: Quakers love silence, madam, and parrots squawk.

ELIZABETH: Oh. *The Way of the World* – is it a comedy?

PARRY: Yes, indeed.

ELIZABETH: I do not care for comedies.

PARRY: *(To MARY.)* You asked me, miss, about the methods the Italians use to train the voice. Well – they're illegal here, of course. But they were available in Bristol.

MARY gasps.

ELIZABETH: *(Very shocked.)* No!

PARRY: And Mr Priest wanted me to have the operation.

ELIZABETH: But – you had your cousin – you went to him?

PARRY: He wanted me to have it too.

ELIZABETH: Worse and worse!

PARRY: They were in alliance. They thought the Welsh Boy could go on making money for them both for years, you see. So Lewis came to me and –

He imitates LEWIS in a strong West Wales accent, throwing himself into the part.

(Sonorous preacher.) 'Some are born eunuchs of women; some are made eunuchs by men; and some make themselves eunuchs for the kingdom of heaven's sake. They that can bear, let them bear.' The Gospel of St Matthew, Chapter Nineteen, Verse Nine. *(Solemn pause, then sales pitch)* You'd earn ten times what any other singer earns, Jemmy. You'd be rich. Very rich. *(Intimate.)* There's a doctor I know, Doctor Rousse, the anatomist, an excellent man, and there's Mr Sam Pye, the surgeon, lives in Clifton – They'd do it. Safely and secretly. And you'd go on singing with that beautiful voice of yours for

years to come. *(Sentimental.)* I had a voice like yours when I was young. And I wish I'd had the operation, I promise you. Women can make a midden of a man's life. *(Pious.)* You'd be spared many temptations to sin. And children, Jem, they're nothing but worry and expense, believe me. *(Intimate.)* I tell you what, seeing as we're cousins, I'll give you a gold watch. With chime. *(He holds up an imaginary watch and makes chiming noise.)* Worth fifty pounds, a watch like that. And just a token of what you'll earn later. You'll be living like a lord. You'll never regret it. *(As himself.)* That was my cousin!

ELIZABETH: *(Has followed the story with intense interest.)* That is the most shocking – But you never –

PARRY: I didn't know what to do. He kept insisting, and Priest kept pressing, and – If it hadn't been for the Donnings, I don't know what might not have happened.

ELIZABETH: Donnings?

PARRY: The family has a large estate in Carolina.

ELIZABETH: Yes, indeed. How did you come to know them?

PARRY: Through my voice, madam. Winifred – *(Quick.)* – and her mother – they heard me singing in the cathedral one day and came to sit in the choir to be near me. Mrs Donning was very kind to me – like the mother I had only ever imagined. I could tell her everything, as I'm telling you now. But they were about to sail for America.

He acts out the scene, playing all three parts.

(Self.) What shall I do without you? You are my only friends in this soulless city! *(WINIFRED.)* He must come with us to America, Mama. *(To MARY and ELIZABETH.)* She was very decisive, Winifred. *(Self, aghast.)* What? *(WINIFRED.)* You can earn a much better living singing in Carolina than you'll ever get here. Can't he, Mama? *(Mrs Donning.)* Oh, yes, no question. *(Self.)* But – Run away from my master? Break my indentures? *(WINIFRED.)* He steals your money as a boy, he wants to rob you of your future as a man – you have every justification. *(Beat, then self.)* Oh,

Winifred – I would rather be with you among Indians and Negroes, than in the finest palaces on earth! *(To the Powells.)* She was like a comet among the common stars!

MARY does not like this at all.

(Dramatizing again.) They were very popular, the Donnings, and the day they were sailing, all the ladies were crying, and – *(Laugh.)* – I had an onion in my handkerchief so people should think how very sad I too was to see them go. I waved and waved, with tears pouring down my cheeks, then it was off to the cathedral for prayers, with my heart beating like the tenor bell, and me singing as if someone had a dagger at my throat. After the service I took off my surplice as calm as could be, then I walked in the Green where people could see me, then I strolled away till it was safe to run, and then I ran as fast as I could to where a yawl was waiting. The men rowed me down the river and out to the ship in the Kings Roads and Winifred hid me in the cabin till the anchor was weighed and then – As the ship went down the channel my heart was light as a cockle!

MARY: She was very pretty, was she, this Winifred Donning?

PARRY: *(Careful.)* I was only fifteen, miss. All women were pretty to me then.

MARY does not like this.

ELIZABETH: One hears so much about America, but I imagine the society is very inferior.

PARRY: Oh, no, madam, it's a very prosperous country, with splendid seats and many good families. They all came to Charlestown to hear me sing.

He sings a snatch.

I liked America very much. I lived like a king.

MARY: I wonder you did not stay there, then. With Miss Donning.

PARRY: I would have done. But Priest was losing money by my absence, he was storming and swearing all over

Bristol, and the dean and chapter were in uproar, and they persuaded the Secretary of War to order the governor of Carolina to take me up and send me home. So when I went one day to teach the daughters of a Charlestown merchant, instead of the girls I found armed men who seized me and put me on board the first ship that was coming home. They had to keep me in chains till we were out of sight of land.

MARY: Like a slave!

PARRY: I'd have jumped overboard otherwise and swum back to shore. But it was all for nothing, for as we were coming back up the Bristol Channel, a great wave broke over the ship – we were just passing Lundy Island – and I was soaked and caught a cold, and when the cold was over my voice had broken. I think it may have been for sorrow at returning.

MARY: Or the loss of Miss Donning?

PARRY: I was indeed very sorry to know the whole vast ocean lay between us. She had been very kind to me.

ELIZABETH: Mr Priest must have been very disappointed if your voice had broken.

PARRY: He was! He gave me dinner, then my indentures, and told me to go where I liked.

ELIZABETH: How old were you then?

PARRY: Still fifteen.

ELIZABETH: I shall write to the bishop about this man!

PARRY: Too late, madam. Priest died last year. Not that I shall ever forget or forgive him.

MARY: And Miss Donning? Do you still think of her?

PARRY: I do, yes. *(Very sad.)* But she too died last year.

ELIZABETH: Oh?

PARRY: She was in a canoe – they're very light craft, canoes – and – I don't know the details. But it overturned and she was drowned.

MARY: *(Pleased.)* How sad.

ELIZABETH: This is an extraordinary story, Mr – May I call you James?

PARRY: My friends call me Jem or Jemmy, madam.

ELIZABETH: *(Thinks.)* I shall call you Jem. So what did you do then?

PARRY: Well, I had sung often enough at Bath, and Mr Nash there knew me, so –

ELIZABETH: *(Impressed.)* Mr Nash? Beau Nash?

PARRY: Yes, madam. He arranged for me to sing in several polite companies, so I was able to get some money. And though my voice had broken, I kept the upper part so strong and clear that no one could tell it from my unbroken one. As I think you will agree.

ELIZABETH: Yes. Yes, indeed.

She ponders a moment.

You have had a sad time of it, Jem, having no mother, and being taken advantage of. But now you have come to a good, quiet place, and you can count on us to help you. To begin with – shall we say, three lessons a week, Mary?

MARY: If that suits Jemmy.

He smiles to acknowledge her use of the name. She smiles back.

ELIZABETH: And after a month we will see what progress you are making. Meanwhile – You are lodging at Widow Apperley's, I understand.

PARRY: Yes, madam.

ELIZABETH: She is very respectable, of course. But her table –

PARRY: *(Shrug.)* A music master cannot pick and choose his victuals.

ELIZABETH: I should be very happy if you were to dine with us today. And on the days you teach Mary. If that would be convenient?

PARRY: *(Bow.)* I should be delighted. When would you like me to begin?

ELIZABETH: Oh, not till the spring. *(Seeing his dismay.)* The spinet is out of tune.

PARRY: I know how to tune a spinet.

MARY: I'm afraid it would go out of tune again as soon as it was mended.

ELIZABETH: Coals are very dear in Ross, Jem. Everything is. So I do not care to have a fire in the room where it is kept. May the first. You can begin on May the first.

PARRY bows, then comes forward to the audience as MARY and ELIZABETH go.

PARRY: Three months before I could see Mary again! Except in church. And not even there to begin with. The rector was not ready for me to begin my duties – so he allowed me to take my diversion in London for a few weeks, going to concerts and operas. I even had the great honour of meeting Mr Handel. But May Day – what better day to start making music? *(Starts to sing Macheath's song from* The Beggar's Opera.*)* 'Youth's the season made for joys'. *(Stops.)* You know *The Beggar's Opera*? It was all the rage in those days, and when they did it at Bath I taught the singers. *(Starts Macheath's song again.)*
Youth's the season made for joys
Love is then our duty.
She alone who that employs
Well deserves her beauty;
Let's be gay, While we may,
Beauty's a flower despised in decay.

*

Let us drink and sport today,
Ours is not tomorrow.

Love with youth flies swift away,
Age is nought but sorrow.
Dance and sing, Time's on the wing,
Life never knows the return of spring.

(Speech, melancholy.) It's true. Life never does know the return of spring. *(Cheering up.)* But Macheath's a wonderful part. All the women are after him. 'I must have women', he says. 'There is nothing unbends the mind like women.' Unbends the mind! And what a true first spring that was! Though it began with a misunderstanding.

He goes to the spinet, and starts tuning it, fixing the strings. MARY comes in, pale, a letter in her hand.

PARRY: A fine May morning, miss! *(Plays a chord.)* The instrument will be ready in a minute.

MARY: There's no need to trouble yourself. I've decided not to take lessons from you after all.

PARRY: *(Taken aback.)* But –

MARY: *(Shows letter.)* This came for you from London this morning.

PARRY: *(Alarmed.)* What? Why –

MARY: The servant at Mrs Apperley's knew you were coming here, so she brought it.

PARRY: Already open?

MARY: I opened it myself. Because I saw it was a woman's hand. And I wished to know what sort of man it was who was proposing to give me lessons.

PARRY: *(To audience.)* Outrageous! But it showed she was more interested in me than music! *(To MARY.)* And what did you discover?

MARY: That you are a libertine!

PARRY: *(Mock bow.)* You do me too much honour.

MARY: Your correspondent – it's signed A.H., but it's obviously a woman – she says – *(Reading.)* – she thought you had died a martyr to love.

PARRY: Does she indeed! May I see?

He tries to grab the letter, but she keeps it out of his reach.

MARY: She insists that on future visits to London you will not only make her house your home, but her bed your own, and her bosom your pillow.

PARRY: *(Still trying to grab it.)* My letter, please, miss.

MARY: So she can rob you of your chastity the first time she sees you. If not her, Judy or Hetty, it seems, are ready to perform the same service.

PARRY: Good! Then you see I am still chaste.

MARY: Foh! If my mother were to see this –

PARRY: *(To audience.)* If she were really shocked she'd have taken that letter straight to her. *(To MARY.)* It's a joke, Mary! A joke by one of my friends. A.H. is Anthony Hughes of Llanarth.

MARY: *(Frown.)* There is no Anthony among the Hugheses of Llanarth. I know them well. They are my cousins.

PARRY: Llanarth in Ceredigion.

MARY: Where?

PARRY: Cardiganshire. Anthony was a choirboy with me at Carmarthen. He sings at Covent Garden now.

She doesn't know whether to believe this. She sniffs the letter.

MARY: This does not smell like a joke. It smells like –

She is suddenly embarrassed by what she was going to say.

PARRY: *(To audience.)* The writer had left her very personal imprint on the paper. As though I needed reminding. *(To MARY.)* The only true thing in all that nonsense is that I am chaste.

He holds out his hand for the letter.

Please?

She still withholds it. He tries again to get it. They grapple. He holds her briefly in his arms. They look close into each other's eyes a moment. Then she thrusts him away.

MARY: What do you think you're doing?

PARRY: Trying to regain my property. But if you wish to keep it, the joke has long since ceased to amuse me, and as my presence here is plainly not to your liking, and there are other young ladies in Herefordshire who are anxious for it, I have no reason to stay where I am not trusted. I wish you good morning.

He goes to pick up his hat.

MARY: No! You mustn't go! What would Mama think?

PARRY: What would she think if she saw that letter? And smelled it? *(Humour.)* If there were only a fire in the room –

MARY: Here. Take it. Dispose of it how you will.

She gives him the letter. He puts it into his pocket.

But if you are to go on coming here, you must promise me something. And you must swear a great oath that you will not only make the promise, but keep it.

PARRY: But if I don't know what the promise is –

MARY: It is something which will be of great service to you.

Their eyes meet. Silence.

Swear to do what I say.

PARRY: *(Beat.)* Very well. I swear to do what you say.

MARY: Never answer that letter. Whether it was written by a friend or not.

PARRY: The writer is no longer my friend.

MARY: Do you swear not to answer it?

PARRY: *(Shrug.)* I swear. What will you promise me in return?

MARY: Oh, you don't know what I shall do for you in time!

She offers him her hand. He bows over it.

PARRY: Shall we begin?

Still keeping her hand, he leads her over to the spinet. They sit side by side.

We hold our hands like this over the keys. No – like this.

She allows him to place her hands. She glances at him, he smiles. Then he goes into a dazzling demonstration of scales and arpeggios. They fade away as he rises and comes to speak to the audience.

The letter was, of course, from a lady of pleasure. One with whom I'd not yet had the pleasure I'd enjoyed with others. My mind had been most thoroughly unbent. *(Laughs.)* Macheath says, 'A man who loves money might as well be contented with one guinea, as I with one woman'. Yet for a long time, with Mary, I was quite content with my one shining guinea. *(Senses the audience's disbelief.)* No, well, she had a very jealous nature, and didn't believe it, either, but – Oh, God, Doomsday.

DOOMSDAY comes on. They are back on the Prospect.

Summer term over already?

DOOMSDAY: Trinity. We call it Trinity term.

PARRY: Oxford vocabulary seems as difficult to grasp as Welsh.

DOOMSDAY: You have to belong to know it, of course. But I must congratulate you, Parry. They tell me you've won the heart of Mrs Powell.

PARRY: *(Startled.)* Mrs Powell?

DOOMSDAY: They say you not only teach the beauteous Mary three times and more a week, but you dine there too, and often stay till midnight.

PARRY: There's a great shortage of acceptable young men in Ross, so I am pressed into service for whist and quadrille, that's all.

DOOMSDAY: They say she treats you almost as the son she never had. A full brother to Mary.

PARRY: She is very kind, yes.

DOOMSDAY: *(Severe.)* They also say that Mr Tudor the curate saw you walking in the garden with your arm round Mary and kissing her in what was not at all a fraternal manner.

PARRY: Mr Tudor saw nothing of the sort. As he has told Madam Powell. Where did you hear all this stuff?

DOOMSDAY: At the Kings Head, as soon as I stepped off the coach.

PARRY: For God's sake! Ross must be the most gossiping place in Britain.

DOOMSDAY: It is. You'll find it's impossible to conduct any sort of private business here without the whole town knowing.

PARRY: Then the sooner the world ends with one tremendous revelation and none of us have a single secret left the better. Can you tell me when that's going to be, exactly? I'd like to make my arrangements.

DOOMSDAY: Where theology and mathematics meet there tend to be sore heads. The debate continues. *(Taking his arm.)* Now – you've done well to win the approval of Mrs Powell. Not an easy woman.

PARRY: She'd be easier if she didn't smoke the whole time. She stinks like a dustwoman!

DOOMSDAY: Yes. But she was a Miss Smith, you know.

PARRY: I suppose many young women were once that.

DOOMSDAY: This one was an only child. Who inherited a very handsome fortune, some of which she used to lend out to such reliable local gentry as Mary's father.

PARRY: Oh?

DOOMSDAY: *(Confidential.)* After his first wife died, he couldn't pay it back, so, for his second he chose – Miss Smith.

PARRY: Ah, a love match! Love of money, anyway.

DOOMSDAY: She was very honoured. The Powells are one of our oldest families. *(Meaning to impress.)* A hundred years ago Mary's grandfather was steward to the Duke of Beaufort.

PARRY: A servile fellow, then.

DOOMSDAY: What the devil do you mean? The Beauforts own half Wales. They go back to the conquest.

PARRY: They do indeed. *(Waving to the view.)* And my whole country is pock-marked with the castles and torture chambers they and their like built to enslave us.

DOOMSDAY: Pooh! That's all history. What matters now is – *(Pointing.)* Great House, Llantilio, is a very comfortable estate. *(Respectfully low.)* Worth five or six thousand pounds.

PARRY: So I have heard.

DOOMSDAY: Which makes Mary a very desirable prize.

PARRY: But it belongs to her brother Matthew, not her.

DOOMSDAY: He's her half-brother, not her brother.

PARRY: What difference does that make? The property is his.

DOOMSDAY: But he has no children. And as his wife is fuddled morning, noon and night, and he prefers to live away from her, in London, there are not like to be. In fact, in my professional medical opinion, even were there to be a highly unlikely reconciliation, husband and wife are both so unhealthy that no issue is probable. She's drinking herself to death, and he not only drinks as much as she does, if not more, he gambles, whores – I give him five years at most. And then, you see, Mary will inherit Llantilio.

PARRY: Hm.

DOOMSDAY: In addition to which, when she's twenty-five, she'll come into a very sizeable inheritance from her father. And – she's her mother's only child, so the Smith money will be hers too, in time. She stands to be very rich indeed.

PARRY: You seem very well informed about the family's finances.

DOOMSDAY: One needs to know what one's doing when one enters the marriage market. Which is where you can help me.

PARRY: I'm afraid I have no means to buy and nothing to sell.

DOOMSDAY: But you've become almost one of the family. And I want you to speak up for me. To Mary.

PARRY is astonished.

If you can persuade her – and her mother – that I would make a suitable husband – I'll give you a hundred – no, two hundred pounds. *(Taps his nose.)* Two hundred gold sovereigns! Verb. sap, Parry, verb. sap!

PARRY: But you – your father – I mean – will she consider – *(Stops, embarrassed.)*

DOOMSDAY: My father is only an attorney, it's true. And attorneys' children cannot usually aspire to such gentry as the Powells. But I am a Balliol man. And I shall soon be a doctor. The only one for miles around with Oxford qualifications. *(False modesty.)* I believe I stand a fair chance. *(Slaps him on the back.)* She's a great prize, Parry! And I mean to capture her! So – will you be my grappling iron? Two hundred pounds worth?

Laughing, he goes. PARRY watches him go, then turns to the audience.

PARRY: Did you ever see such a fool? She'll no more marry him than – *(Grin.)* Last thing in the world – even if its end were truly nigh! But then – what chance had I? *(Strikes a poetic attitude and sings.)*

No flocks have I, no fleecy care,
Nor fields that wave their golden grain;
No pastures green, or gardens fair,
A woman's venal heart to gain.
Then all in vain, my sighs must prove,
Whose whole estate, alas! is love.

But that's nonsense, like most love songs. It's not so
uncommon, is it, for a girl of fortune to choose a husband
for herself, without advice from her relations? To pick
an elegant young man of the spinet rather than a clumsy
second cousin whiffing of the stable? And – a musician
has one great advantage over ordinary men. He speaks
to a woman's heart, not her head. To her feelings, not
her father's or brother's damned attorney. So – here you
behold the jemmy who would crack open her lovely safe!

*He does a little skip, and as he goes to join MARY, who is at the
spinet, she starts playing. He watches a moment, then puts his hand
on her shoulder to stop her.*

Good. Good. But – F sharp there, look, not F natural.

MARY: So it is.

*She plays the phrase again, deliberately getting it wrong. This time
he puts his hand on hers to stop her.*

I'm sorry!

PARRY: *(Both hands over hers.)* Let me guide you. *(They play.)*
You see?

MARY: Yes! It's so much easier when I'm in your hands.

*He takes his hands away and she plays the phrase again, getting it
right, and going on.*

PARRY: *(His hand back on her shoulder.)* Very good!

But now she makes another deliberate mistake, and he stops her.

PARRY: That's a crotchet there, not a quaver.

He sits beside her and plays the phrase correctly.

MARY: Oh. Of course. Show me again.

He covers her hands with his again and they play together.

Yes!

PARRY: Carry on.

*But almost at once, without his hands, she makes another mistake,
and crashes a discord in pretended self-disgust.*

MARY: I'm hopeless!

PARRY: No, no. Compared to Miss White of Goodrich you're a virtuoso.

MARY: Miss White?

PARRY: No ear at all.

MARY: But people think her very pretty.

PARRY: Do they?

MARY: Don't you?

PARRY: *(Beat.)* I cannot judge of a star when I am in the presence of the sun.

Their eyes meet. But the tension is too great, so he breaks it, laughing.

You've no idea of the horrors of a music master's life! Day after day obliged to be polite to insipid provincial misses like the lacklustre Miss White.

MARY: *(Clapping with pleasure.)* Lacklustre!

PARRY: And then my evenings! Last week I had to find an 'orchestra' for the Buckhunters Ball.

MARY: *(Laugh.)* Were they dreadful?

PARRY: There was George Rowlands, the nailer.

MARY: George!

PARRY: Gwyn Jones the shoemaker, and Tom – I don't know his other name – Tom the pedlar.

MARY: *(Delighted.)* How did they play?

PARRY: Oh, with great feeling, all three of them, and all at once. The cacophony was tumultuous.

MARY laughs.

Coming here, Mary, is like coming to heaven after purgatory. *(Beat as she looks down and he thinks he's gone too far.)* Perhaps we'd better try the tune again. A crotchet, remember, not a quaver.

She plays again, making the same mistake.

MARY: I don't know what's the matter with me today!

PARRY: Are you not well? Is it –

MARY: Is it what?

PARRY: *(Unembarrassed.)* My sisters taught me never to press a lady too hard in case she was – it was – 'the custom of women', they called it.

MARY: I'm quite well in that way, thank you. Or I should have sent the servant to tell you not to come.

PARRY: Of course. Shall we try again?

MARY: Though I do have – But it's nothing.

PARRY: What is?

MARY: What is what?

PARRY: The nothing that troubles you.

MARY: Oh, it's just a pimple. But a very annoying one. Just here, you see, where it catches my dress –

She opens her dress to show him a pimple on her upper breast. He looks at it, astonished and delighted.

PARRY: *(Beat.)* It's very small.

MARY: But it's broken just where the embroidery –

PARRY looks at her breast, then into her eyes. Then he touches the pimple gently.

PARRY: Does this make it better?

She gasps. He quickly withdraws his hand.

I'm sorry, I didn't mean to –

MARY: No, no, leave it there. It's – it's very – very soothing.

When he hesitates, she takes his hand and places it firmly on her breast.

Yes, much better. Better at once.

PARRY: Oh, Mary –

He puts his other arm round her neck. They gaze into each other's eyes.

PARRY: Upon your cheek sits lovely youth,

36

Heaven sparkles in your eye,
There's something sweet about your mouth,
Dear Mary, let me try.

MARY: Try what, Mr Poet?

He kisses her. She does not resist. The kiss goes on and on.

PARRY: Oh, Mary, I – I – I – *(To audience.)* That's how we
began. With a pimple! *(Back to MARY.)* You do know I've
loved you, from the moment I first saw you?

A kiss.

MARY: I loved you before that. The day they were choosing
the new organist, I saw you among the other candidates
and prayed and prayed that you –

A kiss.

PARRY: I was talking to that ass Doomsday, when I saw you
with Betty Fisher. You seemed like an angel.

A kiss.

MARY: I couldn't rest till I knew you'd been selected.

A kiss.

PARRY: I've never been in love before. Only read about it. But
when it happens –

A kiss.

MARY: I wouldn't give Mama a moment's peace till she agreed
to let you teach me.

A kiss.

PARRY: As soon as my eyes were blessed with the sight of your
lovely person, I knew that without you, my life would be
unbearable.

A kiss.

MARY: *(Sigh.)* Unbearable!

A kiss.

PARRY: I love you, I love you, I love you!

A long kiss.

MARY: *(Coming up for air.)* What are we going to do?

PARRY: Marry! We must marry and live happily ever after!

MARY: I can't marry without Mama's consent. Not till I'm twenty-five.

PARRY: I can wait. I can wait for ever. Will you – one day – be my wife? Mary?

MARY: I will.

Another long kiss.

We'll marry, and you can give up teaching music, because I'll be rich enough for both of us!

Kiss.

Only –

PARRY: Only what?

MARY: You mustn't go to London and mix with Judies and Hetties.

PARRY: *(Laugh.)* I shall never want any other woman on earth but Mary Powell.

MARY: Oh, Jemmy –

They gaze into each other's eyes a moment then are about to go into another long kiss when –

ELIZABETH: *(Off.)* Mary? Mary?

They quickly resume their positions at the spinet as ELIZABETH enters, rather agitated, a letter in her hand. She stops short, seeing PARRY.

ELIZABETH: Oh. I thought you'd gone, Jem. I heard no music.

PARRY: *(Rising.)* We're just studying some new songs. Looking them over before we play and sing them.

MARY: I'm afraid they may be too difficult for me.

PARRY: No, no. New music always seems daunting at first, but once you get the feel of it –

ELIZABETH: Jem, will you excuse us? I have a family matter to discuss with Mary.

PARRY: Of course.

ELIZABETH: You'll come back for dinner, won't you?

PARRY: That's very kind.

ELIZABETH and MARY go as PARRY comes to the audience and sings.

By the mole on thy bosom, so soft and so white,
By the mole on thy neck, where my arms would unite,
By whatever mole else thou hast got out of sight,
I beseech thee to hear me, dear Molly.

By the kiss just a-starting from off thy moist lips,
By the tip of thy tongue, which all tongues far out-tips;
By the delicate up-and-down jerk of thy hips;
I beseech thee to hear me, dear Molly.

By thy soft downy bosom, on which my soul died;
By thy down of all downs, which I love as my eyes;
By your last thoughts at night, and the first when you rise;
I beseech thee to hear me, dear Molly.

By all the soft pleasures a virgin can share;
By the critical minute no virgin can bear,
By the joys that I languish to ask, but don't dare;
I beseech thee to hear me, dear Molly.

(Speech.) Only of course I didn't languish, I dared. I asked her again and again. And she promised, if I'd only have patience, I could have all the joys a man could dream of. Meanwhile Mrs Powell's news was that Mary's fuddled brother's even more fuddled wife had finally had one too many, and her pickled corpse was to be given a Christian burial at Monmouth. Mary and her mother were to be chief mourners, as Matthew cared so much for the wretched woman that he didn't even bother to come back from London for the funeral. Following which, as he did not like or trust his step-mother, he asked Mary, as his natural heir, to go and manage the Llantilio household

till he felt the need for a month or two of country air to recover from his debauches. So I saw much less of her. And one day, when I did go over to Llantilio –

MARY brings on MATTHEW, a purple-faced roué with something wrong with his palate, so he talks oddly. He cannot see very well, either. He has a glass in his hand. He stops and peers at PARRY.

MATTHEW: Who the devil's this?

MARY: It's Mr Parry, Matthew. My music master. He's been giving me a lesson.

PARRY bows. MATTHEW looks him up and down.

MATTHEW: Egad, these musicians and dancing masters are such damned gaudy fellows, there's no such thing as knowing them from men of fortune!

He and MARY walk on.

PARRY: *(To audience.)* The man could hardly see, nor taste nor smell – some deficiency in his palate. Something even more deficient in his mind – couldn't do the simplest arithmetic. But his real deficiency was in manners.

MATTHEW: *(To MARY.)* That man, the organist – He's not tried to make love to you, has he? Tried to kiss you?

MARY: Matthew! He just teaches me music.

MATTHEW: One hears stories about these fellows. Hoping to take advantage of their pupils.

He sizes her up.

And you're not a girl any longer, are you?

He thrusts his hand into her bosom and feels her breasts. She gasps. PARRY starts forward, as though to hit him, and only just stops himself.

No, by God! You're a woman!

MARY: Mathew!

She tries to get away from him, but MATTHEW is strong. He holds her still and goes on feeling.

PARRY: *(To audience.)* You see that! His own sister! Like feeling a horse's fetlocks!

MATTHEW: Yes! Beginning to look and swell very prettily. *(Removes his hand and pats her on the bum.)* Time I looked out for a husband for you. Some rich but honest Whig, for I hate the damned Tories. Don't want one of those treacherous brutes squeezing your snowy bubbies, do we? They could be worth more than pink diamonds to the right buyer! *(Drinks.)* I might start bargaining for a new wife for myself, while I'm at it. *(Empties the glass.)* Damn! Ambrose! Where is the fellow! Ambrose!

He goes off.

MARY is still gasping. PARRY comes quickly to her. She falls into his arms.

PARRY: My darling – He is the most vile, vicious – I'd like to throttle him!

She rests on his breast a moment, her mind working, then pushes him away.

MARY: Suppose he does find a new wife!

PARRY: What?

MARY: Suppose he marries again! And has a child! I shall be disinherited!

PARRY: *(Beat.)* That won't make any difference to me.

MARY: But it will. I shall only have what my father left me.

PARRY: *(Firm.)* It will make no difference to me. For richer, for poorer, I will always love you.

Beat. She looks at him, wondering. ELIZABETH comes on.

ELIZABETH: Still here, Jem? It's getting dark. You'll want to be off back to Ross.

MARY: Oh, but he was going to give me another lesson, mama –

PARRY: Yes, mama. *(Quick.)* Oh – I beg your pardon, Mrs Powell.

ELIZABETH waves it aside, quite pleased in fact.

ELIZABETH: Not today, I'm afraid. Matthew says – This is Matthew's house, you see, not ours, and he says – You have a warm coat?

PARRY: Yes, madam.

ELIZABETH: Say goodbye, Mary.

MARY: Goodbye, Jemmy.

PARRY: Goodbye. Keep practising those new tunes, won't you?

MARY: I promise.

PARRY: *(Bow to ELIZABETH.)* Madam.

ELIZABETH: Goodbye.

He goes.

Matthew thinks you make too free with Jem, Mary. And now you're growing up –

MARY: But he's like my brother, mama. Much more so than Matthew.

ELIZABETH: Oh, he's a good, honest boy. But –

MARY: I could never think of him in any other way.

ELIZABETH: Well, but you've lived a very sheltered life. You don't know what young men are like. And Matthew takes after your father, he can be so very choleric. *(Frightened, rubbing her chest.)* Practise your music all you like, but while Matthew is here, Jem had better keep away.

She goes, leaving MARY. She begins to sing Scarlatti's sad 'Sento nel Core'.

MATTHEW comes quietly on behind her. He is drunk. He listens a moment, then suddenly puts his arms round her. She gives a startled cry.

MARY: Oh! Matthew!

MATTHEW: Who you singing about?

MARY: What?

MATTHEW: *(Running his hands over her from behind.)* Thinking of your beau, were you? Doctor Dimwit Doomsday, examining you all over with his feely fingers? Oooh!

MARY: Let me go!

MATTHEW: Or was it that fancy Welsh music master?

MARY: Mama! Let me go!

MATTHEW: I've got a piece of news for you.

MARY: Mama!

ELIZABETH comes hurrying on.

ELIZABETH: What's the matter?

MATTHEW: *(Annoyed, letting MARY go.)* Oh, God, she would come interfering!

ELIZABETH: Interfering in what? What's going on?

MATTHEW: I've decided on Mary's future husband.

ELIZABETH: What? Who gave you the right to do that?

MATTHEW: I'm her brother. Her very loving brother.

ELIZABETH: And I'm her mother and as you very well know she can't marry without my consent till she's twenty-five!

MATTHEW: *(Sullen.)* It's a very good match.

ELIZABETH: I shall be the judge of that. Whom are you proposing?

MATTHEW: *(Mocking.)* Whom am I proposing? *(Angry.)* Tom Barker!

MARY, ignored by them both, gives a gasp of horror.

ELIZABETH: But he's sixty!

MATTHEW: All the better for Mary. She won't have to wait long to get his fortune.

ELIZABETH: He's a money-lender!

MATTHEW: So? You used to lend money yourself, didn't you? How you snared my poor father.

ELIZABETH: Your father and I –

MATTHEW: He was up for the highest bidder. And you bought him. Seven hundred pounds, so a grazier's daughter could live here in a gentleman's house as a gentleman's wife, while all the real gentry sneered at you behind your back!

ELIZABETH: You're drunk!

MATTHEW: Very probably. *(Maudlin.)* But don't think I'm blaming you. We're all whores when it comes to marriage. Whores or libertines.

ELIZABETH: Mary! Come with me!

MATTHEW: *(Holding MARY again.)* You stay where you are, Mary. Tom Barker's a very good fellow. Look after you very well. He's kept me going these last ten years. He's going to wipe out all my debts and give me a thousand pounds the day he marries you. Which will be within the month.

MARY: *(Aghast.)* Mama –

ELIZABETH: *(To MATTHEW.)* You have no rights over Mary. She cannot, and will not, marry without my permission.

MATTHEW: She'll do what I tell her!

ELIZABETH: She will do what *I* tell her!

MATTHEW: She'll marry Tom Barker!

ELIZABETH: A poxed extortionate old usurer? Never!

MATTHEW: *(Surprised.)* How do you know he's poxed?

ELIZABETH: All your acquaintance is! I expect you're poxed yourself!

MATTHEW: *(Furious.)* Bitch!

ELIZABETH: Come, Mary! Your brother is out of his senses.

MATTHEW: *(Furious.)* God, you are the most provoking – Get out of my house! You and your simpering harlot of a daughter! Get out!

He makes to strike her, and she cowers away, but he stumbles as he swings his arm and misses. She takes MARY by the hand and they run off together.

Whores, the pair of you! Trollops! Strumpets! Out!

He hurls his glass after them, then staggers off after them.

After a pause, MARY comes back on, with PARRY. He has his arm round her shoulder.

PARRY: Good God, but it was freezing!

MARY: We had to go to the inn. To the Ostrey. We can't go back to Great House, not while he's there. When he drinks – When! He drinks all day, every day! We're a most unhappy family, Jemmy. *(She's been thinking.)* And it's so long till I get the money Papa left me. Anything can happen between now and then. You may change your mind –

PARRY: Never!

MARY: Mama may die and Matthew may find someone else he owes money to –

PARRY: As though you were a brood mare, going to a stallion!

MARY: *(Change of tone, determined.)* I've decided you'd better marry Betty Fisher.

PARRY: *(Staggered.)* What?

MARY: She's a lively, trustworthy girl. She'll make you a very good wife.

PARRY: But there's only one wife I want in the world. And that's you.

MARY: But the world won't want you as my husband.

PARRY: I don't care about the world.

MARY: I do. If we have to live only on what my father left me, and your salary as a music-master – No.

He is shaken. She has it all worked out.

I'll settle six hundred pounds on you the moment I get Papa's money. We'll have an attorney put it in writing. I'll settle another two hundred pounds on Betty's and your first child, and stand godmother to it. If you don't like Betty, there's always Dolly Dew – or Jenny Birch – or –

PARRY: Oh, no shortage of unmarried milliners in Ross, I know! *(Taking her hand.)* But Mary – my dearest, my only Mary. After all the vows that have passed between us, how can you ask me to make love to another – any other – woman? If each of those mantua-makers had a million pounds, I still wouldn't marry one. *(Moves his hand to her breast.)* Here is where my love is rooted. Heaven can witness that it is you and only you I love, or ever can love, on earth.

She looks at him a long moment, then lets him kiss her. Then she breaks away, laughing.

MARY: If you'd agreed to marry Betty, I'd never have spoken to you again! But if you can really still want to marry me, without my fortune –

PARRY: If you think – if anyone thinks – it is your fortune I am after – I will have writings drawn whereby you shall always be mistress of it after marriage, to do with as you please, and I will sign them and have them witnessed. All I've ever wanted is you. My darling Mary.

They kiss.

MARY: Still – Matthew has made Mama suspicious. So I want you – really this time – to write a love-letter to Celia Deane.

PARRY: *(Astonished.)* What? A serving woman?

MARY: She comes from a very respectable family. Her father's a clergyman in Worcester.

PARRY: She's still a serving woman.

MARY: Well, but you're only a music master. *(He winces.)* And you won't actually have to marry her. It's only to put Mama off the scent.

PARRY: I can't write a false love-letter. I can only say what I feel to one person in the world, and that's you.

MARY: I know. And I love you for it. So – here.

She hands him a book with the place marked.

PARRY: *God's Revenge Against Murder?*

MARY: It's a letter-book. I've marked the place, look.

PARRY: *(Reading.)* 'Madam, The sweetness of your beauty, and the excellency of your virtues, have so fully taken up my thoughts, and so firmly surprised and vanquished my heart – ' This is pure flim-flam.

MARY: Flummery. But isn't love easy to pretend? Go on.

PARRY: ' – that I am so much yours, both by conquest and duty, as I know not whether I do more affect or honour, or more admire or adore you.' She'll think I'm stark staring mad.

MARY: Well, we don't want her to believe it, do we? It's not for her, it's for Mama to think your interest lies anywhere but with me. Write it out and I'll get the servant to deliver it.

PARRY: But I hardly know her!

MARY: That's why it's such a good idea. Mama will think you're mad with love, but Celia will think you're simply mad.

PARRY becomes CELIA DEANE and acts out her anger.

PARRY: This is pure shiddle come shite! James Parry is a blockhead! A sorry scoundrel! An organ-playing piper! Neither a boy nor yet a man, and too stupid to be either!

He tears an imaginary letter into pieces and scatters them. MARY laughs, then looks through the book.

MARY: There's a second letter here for when she rejects the first. It's even more high-flown.

PARRY: Two letters!

MARY: We've got to make it convincing, Jemmy.

PARRY: *(To audience.)* And apparently it was. People were sorry for me, being so in love, and Celia so adamant against me,

47

and it fooled Mrs Powell so successfully she started looking for a bride for me herself among the multitude of milliners.

ELIZABETH comes on, thoughtful. MARY watches.

ELIZABETH: What do you think to Dolly Dew?

PARRY: She – she's charming, in her way, but –

ELIZABETH: Janet Lane?

PARRY: I understand she's already committed.

ELIZABETH: Margaret Evans?

PARRY: Rather too forceful. To say the truth, madam, I feel the sudden passion I had for Miss Deane, and the speed with which it came and went, shows how I am not yet old enough to marry. Besides, I couldn't even afford the wedding breakfast.

ELIZABETH: I mean to give you that. We shall have half a dozen dishes of different meats. You need meat at a marriage. And pies and puddings beside.

PARRY: You're extraordinarily kind.

ELIZABETH: I'm very fond of you, Jem. You just let me know when you're ready, and whom you've decided on, and I will do the rest. Provided I like the girl, of course.

She goes.

PARRY: *(To audience.)* She never even considered that Mary and I might be in love. I was a mere music master. Mere! People kept saying mere! Sometimes even Mary said it.

MARY: You've been seeing a lot of Mary Hill!

PARRY: I've seen her precisely three times.

MARY: Four, I think.

PARRY: Only if you include church.

MARY: You can see where she and her aunt sit from the organ loft.

PARRY: Good God, have you measured the angles from my loft to every seat in the church? Is there anywhere I'm allowed to look?

MARY: I want you to stop seeing Mary Hill. In church or out.

PARRY: But why?

MARY: She says you've been teaching her songs.

PARRY: Yes. She's got a beautiful voice, but untrained. She sings entirely by ear. So I –

MARY: The Italian songs you taught me.

PARRY: Her voice is pitched very like yours. Not nearly so sweet, but –

MARY: You said you brought those songs for me. For me alone.

PARRY: Music is for everyone, Mary.

MARY: Not those songs. I don't want you teaching Miss Hill another note of them. Or of anything else. I don't want you ever to see her again.

PARRY: This is foolishness. I love you, you know how much. And she's only here another week.

MARY: I suppose you've been trying to persuade her to stay longer!

PARRY: *(Beat.)* Your voice is not so very sweet today, Mary.

MARY: But I'm risking everything for you! My name, my reputation, my – While you, a mere music master, go about, without a care in the world, talking to every pretty girl you meet! Not that I'd call Mary Hill even halfway pretty. But can't you see how that must hurt me?

PARRY: But I've sworn to be faithful to you! Again and again. And I've kept my oath. Why won't you believe me?

MARY: Because I cannot bear to see you with another woman.

PARRY: Then, for God's sake, let's get married! Tomorrow! And be done with all this fiddle-faddle and pretence!

MARY: I can't marry without my mother's consent! Not for five years!

PARRY: We can marry secretly.

MARY: *(Ignores that.)* Promise me you won't see her again.

PARRY: *(Weary.)* All right. I promise. I was going to Hereford for the music making next week, anyway. I'll go a few days early.

MARY: And leave me here alone? While you gawp at the Hereford ladies?

PARRY: For heaven's sake!

He goes to the spinet and takes his frustration out on it, then leaps up and addresses the audience.

One day I happened to meet a fellow Welshman at the Post Office – Ross is on the way from Carmarthen to London, and I like to hear the news of my home country. He challenged me to a game of fives in the churchyard, with battle-boards. I was just going to fetch the boards when I saw Dolly Dew on her way to her father's shop.

DOLLY DEW starts to cross the stage.

I liked her much better than I told Mrs Powell, and Mary had been very wearisome that morning, so –

He comes up behind DOLLY DEW and catches her round the waist. She squeaks.

DOLLY: Oh, Mr Parry!

PARRY: Oh, Dolly! You have the ripest lips in England, so soft, so red – they're redder than cider apples. Oh, God, it makes me drunk just to see them – yes, my head is swimming – I shall faint – to be so near and not kiss them – I shall die, Dolly, I shall die if you don't let me –

MARY has come on in time to see and hear the last of this, as DOLLY willingly lets him have his way. The kiss goes on and on. MARY turns on her heel and marches off. PARRY sees her and breaks away.

PARRY: Oh, dear. We seem to have upset Miss Powell.

DOLLY: Miss Powell! You men may think she's wonderful, but us girls, we've known her all our lives, and if it wasn't for her mother, she'd be the most stuck-up creature in Herefordshire and Monmouthshire combined! Here!

She grabs him and gives him another kiss.

Laughing, PARRY breaks away. As DOLLY goes, he crosses to where MARY is waiting for him. She aims a blow at him which he dodges.

MARY: You wretch! You hound! Thank God I've found you out in time!

PARRY: For heaven's sake, what harm is there in giving a modest girl a simple kiss?

MARY: Modest! When you had one hand round the slut's waist and the other round her neck! If that's modesty – !

PARRY: She's not a slut, she's –

MARY: But what else could I expect from a cheat and scoundrel like you!

PARRY: *(Furious.)* Don't you call me a scoundrel!

MARY: Beggar! Vagabond! You're nothing but a Welsh vagabond!

PARRY: Me a vagabond! When your drunken brother throws you out of the house in the middle of the night to wander the frozen lanes! Who was the vagabond then?

MARY: Louse! You lying, cozening louse!

PARRY: How dare you!

He is about to hit her, and she cowers away.

Hell and damnation!

He thinks better of it and starts to storm off.

MARY: Don't you go! I haven't finished with you yet!

PARRY: Go to the devil!

MARY: Jemmy!

PARRY: And take your tobacco-stained mother with you!

He's gone.

MARY: *(Regretting her anger.)* Jem! Jem! Jemmy!

She hurries after him.

PARRY reappears, still fuming.

PARRY: I'm a Welshman, and we Welsh are passionate, and if she'd been a man – I will not stand for being called names. Taffy, the English sneer – *(Lahdidah English accent.)* Taffy was a Welshman, Taffy was a thief! *(Own voice.)* They're the thieves. When they came to Wales, they didn't just steal our sheep, they stole everything, even the mountains the sheep grazed on. And they won't give them back while there's a copper coin still to be stolen. If Owen Glendower had lived –

MARY comes running on after him.

MARY: Jemmy!

He turns his back on her.

(In tears.) Jemmy – dear, dear Jem – *(She falls to her knees.)* For God's sake forgive me for being so wicked – calling you names – from the bottom of my heart, I apologise.

PARRY: *(To audience, quoting grandly.)* 'What cold determination can't the tears of weeping beauty melt? Love in gaiety may affect us, but only love in mourning truly wounds the heart.' *(Drops to his knees beside her.)* Mary – Mary – Please get up. Please.

MARY: Not till you swear the greatest oath you can think of, that you do sincerely forgive me.

PARRY: May the Almighty, here and now on this very spot, strike me dead if I do not forgive my beloved with all the sincerity that one Christian can forgive another.

He raises her up.

MARY: Oh, Jemmy!

PARRY: My sweet, I beg you – if my simple kissing of Dolly Dew was really so disagreeable to you – *(She sobs.)* I promise never ever to kiss any other lips but your softest own.

She kisses him.

MARY: Thank you. And as you have been so good to forgive me, I – I will deny you nothing in the world that you shall ask me.

He is not sure what she means.

If it is in my power to grant it.

PARRY: Do you truly mean that?

MARY: *(Lowered eyes.)* I do.

PARRY: *(Taking her in his arms.)* Then give me yourself. Because there is nothing this side of the grave I desire so much. If you will, I will get a licence, a ring, and a parson immediately.

MARY: *(Firm, but staying in his arms.)* No parson on earth can marry us yet. But – We love each other to distraction, don't we?

PARRY: By all the saints in heaven, yes!

MARY: Then I will let you enjoy me.

He is speechless with delight.

Only we must first read the marriage service over to ourselves, so we are man and wife in the sight of heaven.

PARRY: Oh, Mary – Mary –

MARY: *(Has it all thought out.)* We'll do it tomorrow, while Mama is at church. I will pretend to be out of order, so I can't go with her.

She produces a ring and a prayer-book.

PARRY: *(Overjoyed, but laughing, to audience.)* Another example of the custom of women? To take all the breath from a man's body with surprise and delight? *(To MARY.)* A ring!

MARY: It's one Mama lost seven years and more ago. Then someone found it in a dunghill and she gave it to me.

PARRY: Would she not be – surprised at the way you mean to use it?

MARY: I love Mama, but I am not ruled by her. My heart and mind are my own. *(Solemn.)* Will you begin, my dearest?

PARRY: *(Treating the audience as a congregation.)* Dearly beloved, we are gathered together here in the sight of God and in the face of this congregation, to join together this man and this woman in holy matrimony, which is an honourable estate, instituted of God in the time of man's innocency...

MARY: I require and charge you both, as ye will answer at the dreadful day of judgement when the secrets of all hearts shall be disclosed, that if either of you know any impediment, why ye may not be lawfully joined in matrimony...

They look at each other, both knowing the impediments.

Wilt thou have this woman to thy wedded wife?

PARRY: I will. Wilt thou have this man to thy wedded husband?

MARY: I will.

PARRY: With this ring I thee wed.

MARY: With my body I thee worship. And with all my worldly goods I thee endow.

PARRY: Those whom God hath joined together, let no man put asunder.

They look at each other, very solemnly. They kiss gently. Then with more passion; and yet more. They begin to unbutton each other furiously. Then PARRY stops, remembering the audience.

You still here? Then, while I possess all that my soul has longed for, I suggest you go for a drink. *(To lighting box.)* Lights down!

Blackout.

ACT TWO

JAMES PARRY comes strolling on, a very happy grin on his face.

PARRY: You can't help smiling, can you? When the weather suddenly changes and you open the door, and instead of the sleety sting of March it's the soft kiss of an April sun. Yesterday everything was dreary shades of drab, today the colours are singing louder even than the birds. And – and – and – And falling in love is wonderful, of course. But there's better later, there's best, isn't there, when you hold your girl in your arms for the first time, and worship her with your body, and she worships you with hers – that's something altogether else. Your whole self is singing. Not just the obvious parts, swollen with joy, but toes and fingers, knees and elbows, hair – yes, even your hair. When I was a choirboy in Carmarthen, the choirmaster, Mr Edwards, he told me to sing through the top of my head. Let the music rise from the pit of your stomach, he said, let it pass up through your lungs and throat, and when it reaches your mouth, don't let it escape there, make it go on rising, up through your nose, your sinuses, your brows, till it soars through the roof of your skull and on up through your hair towards heaven. Then, he said, then you are the music and the music is you. I've loved music all my life, but I've only rarely felt that. When I have – it's rapture. And with Mary Powell I felt rapture again and again. *(Sings.)*

Were I laid on Greenland's coast, And in my arms embraced my lass; Warm amidst eternal frost, Too soon the half year's night would pass.

MARY appears to join in the song. She has a copy of his book in her hand.

And I would love you all the day –

MARY: Every night would kiss and play –

PARRY: If with me you'd fondly stray –

MARY: Over the hills and far away –

Repeat last part, ending together.

Over the hills and far away!

They kiss. MARY breaks away.

MARY: *(Tapping his book.)* All that is true. The rapture was
genuine, mine as well as his. In fact mine may have been
the greater. I had lived all my life till then under severe
restrictions as Miss Powell of Llantilio Crossenny. But
now I was Mary Powell as well, with my own secret life,
my blood tingling all day with the memory of my last –
encounter! – with Jemmy, and with trembling anticipation
of the next. I was in a daily delirium of joy. But I had to
be very careful that my mother had no inkling of what
was going on, or – Well! Do you know the Duchess of
Malfi? It's a horrid play about a high-born lady who
falls in love with a man from a lower social order, and is
brutally tortured and killed by her brothers for her daring.
I kept reading it, over and over, revolted by its cruelty
but fascinated by the Duchess, who had the courage to
follow her own feeling, and to refuse to be what other
people wanted. I didn't expect my mother to murder me
for loving Jemmy, but my brother might, and I knew all
the Duchess's excitement at the terrible risks involved.
They were heady days. But though I happily sang along
with Mr Parry to that tune of love fulfilled, his version
of events is different from mine. The motto of Captain
Macheath, whose song that is, was – 'How happy could
I be with either, were t'other dear charmer away!' So my
reasons for jealousy were well-founded. *(Beat.)* I strongly
dislike *The Beggar's Opera*. The men are libertines whom
we're supposed to admire, and the women are whores
whom we're supposed to despise. Neither of them knows
anything of real love, they merely exchange bodies for
money. 'Suits of love', says one of the thieves, 'are won
by pay, and beauty must be fee'd into men's arms'. And
the audience laughs and agrees. The audience of men.
But I do not laugh. If you're a woman with a fortune of
your own, or are like to get one, the roles are reversed.

The men pursuing us are offering their bodies in return
for our money. Which makes them the whores and us
the libertines, something Mr Parry neglects to observe.
(Beat.) Do you know *The Maid's Tragedy* by Beaumont and
Fletcher? That's a play I like. It too is about libertines,
and is full of jokes about wedding nights and so on. But –
though it's written by men – it's truthful about the way they
treat women over whom they have power. Which is not
what the men in the audience then or now want to hear, so
it's not played much.

(Reciting.) There is a vile dishonest trick in man,
More than in women. All the men I meet
Appear thus to me, are harsh and rude,
And have a subtlety in everything,
Which love could never know; but we fond women
Harbour the easiest and the smoothest thoughts,
And think all shall go so. It is unjust
That men and women should be matched together.

(Ordinary speech.) Jemmy didn't like it when I quoted that.
He denied any subtlety in himself, he simply said –

PARRY: I love you. What more can I say? I love you with all
my heart.

MARY: And I loved him. So –

(Sings.) Were I sold on Indian soil,
Soon as the burning day was closed,
I could mock the sultry toil,
When on my charmer's breast reposed.

PARRY: And I would love you all the day –

MARY: Every night would kiss and play –

PARRY: If with me you'd fondly stray –

MARY: Over the hills and far away.

Repeat chorus.

PARRY: We loved with such violence, that it was as though a spell had been laid on us. Enjoyment was so far from palling my desires, it rather increased them.

MARY: And mine!

PARRY: We lived in all the delights of love, and gave ourselves up so entirely to it, that we thought of nothing –

MARY: But each other!

PARRY: Are you telling this story or am I?

MARY: We both are!

PARRY: Well – but no joy is ever quite unconfined. You were still enraged if I so much as spoke to another woman in the street.

MARY: Yes, but you –

PARRY: And if you were jealous, so was I.

MARY: *(Laughing.)* Of Doomsday!

PARRY: I know, I know, he was a pompous Oxford noodle, BA, MA and MB soon to be. *(To audience.)* But he had offered me two hundred pounds to help him marry Mary and two hundred pounds – well, it meant he was serious. And he was friends with Dr Morgan, a Ross surgeon busy killing off his patients with poisonous potions at a guinea a pot. And Dr Morgan had spoken very slightingly of me in front of some of my friends, as a 'mere' – of course 'mere' – Welsh music master, and now he and his wife were having a private dancing-match, and Mary was invited, and Doomsday, but not mere me. *(To MARY.)* I don't want you to go.

MARY: Oh, but I love dancing, and there's so little entertainment here.

PARRY: By the love I bear you and you bear me, I entreat you not to go.

MARY: You can't possibly be jealous of Doomsday!

PARRY: He wants to marry you.

MARY: Wants! He can go on wanting – till doomsday!

PARRY: Besides – can't you imagine how painful it is for me to hear other people talking about you as though you were still – unattached? I've sworn to marry you. Do you not still want to marry me?

MARY: Of course I do. I've told you a thousand times. If you stay in Ross and remain constant to me, and love me as you have done, I will marry you. But I don't see why –

PARRY: When?

MARY: Soon.

PARRY: Swear it.

MARY: I swear.

PARRY: *(Kissing her.)* I love you.

MARY: And I love you.

PARRY: Then please don't go to the Morgans'.

MARY: Oh, very well, then! I won't!

The kiss is prolonged, then PARRY breaks away.

PARRY: *(To audience.)* But she did, damn it!

MARY: *(To audience.)* And why shouldn't I have done? Night after night, when he wasn't playing cards with us, he went to taverns. Why shouldn't I go dancing once in a while?

She dances off, passing ELIZABETH coming on.

PARRY: I was so sure she had not gone, I came to her Mama's at nine o'clock that night for our usual whist.

ELIZABETH: No cards tonight, Jem, Mary's gone to the Morgans'. They're having a dance, you know, in the town hall.

PARRY: I do know, madam Powell, and I am sorry to tell you I do not think the company is suitable for Mary.

ELIZABETH: Why ever not?

PARRY: *(Spur of the moment.)* There are men there – I will not call them gentlemen – men of atheistic morals.

ELIZABETH: *(Alarmed.)* Who can you mean?

PARRY: Surgeons, madam, are always cutting people open and rummaging around inside them. And then they say they cannot find the human soul.

ELIZABETH: Oh, don't be so foolish! Mr Morgan is my own doctor. And he never misses church.

PARRY: I wish you would send for Mary to come home.

ELIZABETH: No, no. It's kind of you to tell me your doubts, Jem, but Mary has promised to be home by eleven. Doomsday, as you call him, is going to be there. He'll see no harm comes to her, I'm sure.

Smiling, she goes.

PARRY: *(To audience.)* Doomsday! Damned man! I went to drink his ill health at an inn.

(Sings.) Fill every glass, for wine inspires us,
And fires us with courage, love and joy.
Women and wine should life employ.
Is there aught else on earth desirous?

But after a few glasses the thought of him linking arms with her, pressing his suit quite literally against her – *(Imitation.)* You're looking a little feverish, Mary, I think I should feel your pulse – what a delightful wrist! – how Oxford would admire it! – yes, yes, raised, definitely raised – will you allow me? – your temperature – as I feared – may I loosen your stays? Perhaps if you stepped out of your dress altogether – *(Own voice.)* Doctors! Professional feelers of intimate female flesh! I couldn't bear it! I had to go and hear what was going on.

'Old Barnaby' *on harp, sound of dancing and clapping and people having a good time.*

Ned Williams the barber on his barbarous harp! He only knew the one tune – 'Old Barnaby'.

MARY: *(Off.)* Again! Let's have it again!

Music starts again.

PARRY: Mary! Enjoying herself without me! I was – I was vexed. I was very, very vexed.

He looks round for something to throw, picks up a piece of wood and hurls it at the sound. There is the crash of the wood against a wall. Sudden silence.

DOOMSDAY: *(Off.)* What the devil was that?

MARY: *(Off.)* The house is falling down! Help!

PARRY: *(To audience.)* But she knew at once it was me.

Shouts, cries of panic. Then MARY comes running across the stage, with DOOMSDAY day after her.

DOOMSDAY: Mary! It's nothing! Come back! Mary!

PARRY watches them disappear with satisfaction.

PARRY: That stopped that. But I was still so vexed I drank a good deal more to calm my vexation, only that seemed to make it worse and – *(Sings* 'All Through the Night', *drunkenly and in Welsh.)*

Holl amrantau'r sêr ddywedant
Ar hyd y nos
Dyma'r ffordd i fro gogoniant
Ar hyd y nos
Golau arall yw tywyllwch
I arddangos gwir brydferthwch
Teulu'r nefoedd mewn tawelwch
Ar hyd y nos.

O mor siriol, gwena seren
Ar hyd y nos –

(Breaks off.) All through the night! I couldn't sleep, thinking of Mary in the arms of Balliol. And when I went round early next morning to tongue-claw her for her breach of promise, and found Doomsday there before me –

MARY and DOOMSDAY have come back on. They look at him in astonishment, as he has to cling to the nearest object to stand upright.

So, madam, you went dancing last night, though your promised me not to! *(Attempts a mocking bow and nearly falls over.)* I must thank you for favouring such an elegant company with your presence!

MARY: For shame, Mr Parry! You've been drinking!

PARRY: And if I have, you drove me to it, by mixing with people who would gladly murder me!

DOOMSDAY: My dear fellow –

PARRY: You prefer the company of a parcel of poor mantua makers and their even poorer followers –

MARY: *(Firm.)* Would you mind stepping into the kitchen? My mother would like a word with you.

PARRY: I want no word with her. You can both go to the –

DOOMSDAY: Parry!

But PARRY is already staggering off.

I'm afraid, Mary, you should be less friendly with Parry. Not being a varsity man, he doesn't know how to carry his liquor. And – *(Lower.)* People say he's ruined his voice with drinking and –

He stops, embarrassed to say 'whoring'.

I'll have a word with him when he's sober.

He follows PARRY off.

MARY: *(Sigh, to audience.)* As though there was not enough drinking in my own family! And it was not the first time he'd behaved like that. He was becoming notorious in our straight-laced little town. So why did I not break it off there and then? Because – aren't we all cowards in love matters? Don't we all do everything to keep love going, smooth and easy, hoping things will turn out for the best? I did. And whatever our disagreements in public, when we were alone the music we made was – divine. I knew his faults, knew them better than he did himself. But – I loved him. I thought it was absence from me that made him drink. I thought, if our love could only be open and declared, he would stop at once.

She goes as PARRY and DOOMSDAY come back on together, PARRY now sober.

DOOMSDAY: Pox take you for a mad dog, what on earth got into you?

PARRY: I had a pain in my head. I took a dram or two against it.

DOOMSDAY: That is an explanation of, not an excuse for, your behaviour.

PARRY: Well, I don't like Dr Morgan. I don't like Mary going there.

DOOMSDAY: What business is it of yours where she goes? She's perfectly capable of choosing her company for herself. And Morgan's a good fellow. As soon as I'm qualified, I mean to go into partnership with him.

PARRY: So the two of you can finish off the few townspeople he hasn't managed to kill on his own!

DOOMSDAY: As a matter of fact – you must keep this to yourself, please –

(Important.) I've been buying myself a new suit of clothes.

PARRY: Really?

DOOMSDAY: With frosted buttons.

PARRY: Very foppish for a doctor, surely?

DOOMSDAY: An Oxford man is permitted to be a little exquisite. And the tailor said – word seems to have got about before I wanted – he said if it was true I was getting married, then he recommended I had the suit lined with white shagreen. So I told him to get on with it.

PARRY: Getting married? To whom?

DOOMSDAY: Mary, of course.

PARRY: *(To audience.)* As I feared. But he didn't know I'd sprung that mine already. *(To DOOMSDAY.)* I hope you'll ask me to the wedding.

DOOMSDAY: Of course, my dear fellow.

PARRY: I'll buy you a present out of the two hundred pounds you'll owe me.

DOOMSDAY: *(Alarmed.)* Oh –

PARRY: Because I've been working on your behalf with Mary every day for months.

DOOMSDAY: Very kind, I'm sure, but –

PARRY: You're not going to renege on your promise?

DOOMSDAY: No, no, of course not. A Balliol man never reneges.

PARRY: If you haven't got the money, you can pay me out of the fortune Mary brings you.

DOOMSDAY: *(Lofty.)* I am not in the least concerned with Mary's portion. It is she I love, not her money.

PARRY: Of course. I wish you joy of both.

DOOMSDAY: Thank you.

DOOMSDAY goes.

PARRY: *(To audience.)* He was a ninny, of course. But if he fancied his chances with Mary, so would every fortune-hunter in the country. And Mary had so little protection. She and her brother were reconciled, and Matthew had gone back to his London orgies, leaving her in charge at Llantilio again. And since her mother stayed in Ross, Mary was alone. Fifteen filthy winter miles away from me.

ELIZABETH comes on.

Though of course, when I could get over there, it was pure idyll. *(Laugh.)* Her mother had not the smallest idea how often that was!

ELIZABETH: You will come and dine today, won't you, Jem? Betty Fisher and Dolly Dew are coming to play quadrille.

PARRY: I can't stay late, I'm afraid. I have to teach in Abergavenny tomorrow morning.

ELIZABETH: Oh? Teach whom?

PARRY: A Miss Jones. *(To audience.)* There was, of course, no Miss Jones in Abergavenny. Well, I dare say there were a hundred. But I was not teaching any of them. I'd put an advertisement in the newspaper, just to deceive Mrs Powell, offering my services throughout Monmouthshire. Then I could pretend I was in Abergavenny or Newport or Llanvihangel Torymynnydd, when in fact I was tuning the spinet, as you might say, in Llantilio. But there were harsh notes there as well as sweet ones.

MARY is coming on, in a panic. He tries to embrace her but she pushes him away.

Is something the matter, my angel?

MARY: Oh, God, I've been in absolute terror!

PARRY: But of what, child?

MARY: Oh, good God, of just that – a child! The flowers were three days late and I thought they were never coming! I took five infusions of dittany before – Culpepper's Directory says nothing of it taking so long to work, I thought – What did I not think?

PARRY: *(Embracing her.)* Then we must put it off no longer. We must get married properly. Now.

MARY: Impossible. My mother –

PARRY: But suppose you do have a child. You don't want it to be a bastard. Think of the disgrace – for you, and the babe.

MARY: Oh, God, I've been thinking of nothing else!

PARRY: But if we can show we are married –

MARY: Matthew will kill me if I marry you.

PARRY: I'll kill him first.

MARY: *(Beat, ignoring that.)* I will marry you, Jemmy. I promise. But not now. Not yet.

PARRY: When, then?

MARY: *(At random.)* Oh – Next summer. I promise.

PARRY: But that's months away!

MARY: The time will pass soon enough. *(To audience.)* 'Next summer' was like saying, Over the hills and far away. We all say things like that, don't we, easily, smoothly, giving in to the overwhelming sweep of love?

PARRY: *(Embracing her.)* I hate to think of you all alone here. I shall write to you every day.

MARY: *(Practical.)* Oh, that would never do. The post boys tell everyone who gets what letters. We'd be discovered at once.

PARRY: But if I can't see you, I must tell you somehow how much I love you. I tell you what, I'll send you music, and in the blank parts of the score I'll write what I feel in lemon juice which you can warm in front of the fire when there's no one there.

MARY: *(Enjoying this.)* Urine's better! It's what they use in old plays! Then I can imagine the source of the invisible ink!

PARRY: My sweetheart!

Excited embrace. Then MARY goes.

PARRY: *(To audience.)* The winter dragged on, the lanes no more than ditches, the girls' voices ever shriller with the cold and wet, with only my swift and secret visits to the raptures of Llantilio to warm me. And – I confess, I'm one of those men who can't be without a woman long, which can be a mighty inconvenience when you're conducting a secret love affair. If Mary had known where my mind sometimes led me, her suspicions would have been well-founded. But I stayed faithful. Truly. I was hers, and hers alone. *(As though to a challenge from the audience.)* You can believe her if you wish, madam, but I tell you I was faithful to my beloved. As she was to me. Though her temptations were hardly as exciting as my own. I mean – her second cousin, Dicky Jeffries!

He watches as ELIZABETH is coming on with her cousin, the red-haired MRS JEFFRIES. DICKY trails behind them, grinning foolishly.

Look at the booby! But his carroty mother, she was danger.

ELIZABETH: *(Cold.)* It is always a pleasure to see you and Dicky, of course, cousin.

PARRY: *(To audience.)* The petty gentry of Monmouthshire are all related to each other. It's astonishing their children aren't all born with two heads.

ELIZABETH: But to what do I owe the pleasure of this visit? Has the winter been so very hard in your part of the country that you have come to seek comfort in Ross? Has the roof of your – *(Deliberately offensive pause as she seeks for the right word.)* – your dwelling finally collapsed?

PARRY: *(To audience.)* It was a dirty hole of a hovel in Penrhos.

MRS JEFFRIES: Dear me, no. We are as comfortable as ever.

ELIZABETH sneers.

We were hoping to see Mary.

ELIZABETH: She's at Great House. Matthew has decided she would be a better steward than the rogue who had the place there.

MRS JEFFRIES: So she is learning how to be a good wife.

ELIZABETH glares.

Is she thinking then of a husband?

ELIZABETH: Girls think of little else at her age.

MRS JEFFRIES: She's twenty-four, isn't she?

ELIZABETH: Not yet twenty-two.

MRS JEFFRIES: Getting on, though. Has she – have you – anyone in mind?

ELIZABETH: She has followers. But she shows no sign of caring for any of them in the way of marriage.

MRS JEFFRIES: If she can't make up her mind – And since they are cousins –

She looks at DICKY who grins.

And have known each other for so long –

ELIZABETH: Dicky? I don't know that Mary has ever been fond of him in that way.

MRS JEFFRIES: He's very fond of her. Aren't you, Dicky?

He grins again.

And – forgive my saying this, Elizabeth, but there's so much gossip about Mary and her music master, I thought you'd like to –

ELIZABETH: Gossip is gossip and nothing else.

MRS JEFFRIES: Yes, but people do say –

ELIZABETH: People will say anything. Mr Parry had a very sad upbringing and we have been kind to him, that is all. He is very good company for me as well as Mary. He plays a good hand at quadrille. But he understands his position.

MRS JEFFRIES: Dicky can play quadrille, can't you, Dicky?

DICKY: *(Alarmed.)* Whist. I can play whist.

MRS JEFFRIES: *(Cross with him.)* I taught you quadrille, remember?

He looks blank.

ELIZABETH: I'm afraid, cousin, that Mary would not care to live in Penrhos. In your – dwelling.

MRS JEFFRIES: Oh, but with her fortune, they could live anywhere.

PARRY: *(To audience.)* It's money makes the mare to go!

ELIZABETH: Oh, if it's money you're after! Good morning!

She goes, very haughty.

DICKY: Am I going to marry Mary then, Mama?

MRS JEFFRIES: *(Tidying him up.)* We shall see.

DICKY: She's got lovely titties.

MRS JEFFRIES: *(Slapping him.)* I told you not to use that word! And look at you! Clean breeches only this morning, and muck on them already! What's she going to think of that? I've told you a thousand times, with people like Cousin Powell, you must wash!

DICKY: I washed my face before we started.

MRS JEFFRIES: I mean, wash all over!

DICKY: *(Appalled.)* All over! In April!

MRS JEFFRIES: *(Sigh.)* Come along!

They go, as ELIZABETH comes on again with MARY.

ELIZABETH: There is too much gossip about you, Mary. I don't mean about Jem. That, we know, is nonsense. But if cousin Jeffries imagines Dicky is a suitable husband for you –

MARY laughs.

It's no laughing matter. There's Doomsday, too. And I don't know how many others. A woman in your position, with no father but good prospects, needs to be very careful whom she chooses. I had to be, when my father died.

MARY: Is that why you married a man so much older than yourself?

ELIZABETH: *(Awkward.)* There was no one I loved better. There was, to be honest, no one I loved at all. Whatever love may be. Nor did anyone love me, though one or two pretended. But there were several men who lusted after my money. I certainly didn't want any of those. I'd known your father for some years, we had a business arrangement – I thought he would be – safe. And give me a decent position in the county.

MARY: And was he not safe?

ELIZABETH: Till he needed more money, yes. Then he wanted me to break my settlement so he could get possession of my fortune. Naturally I refused. I had to defend myself. So – Have you never wondered why I smoke so much? When I know you hate the smell?

MARY: You've always said it soothed you.

ELIZABETH: Well, it does. Though as a matter of fact I hated tobacco at first. But when I refused your father, he – It's very uncomfortable to tell you this. He was so ashamed afterwards, he made me promise never to tell anyone, and to this day I never have, but – *(Beat.)* He struck me. *(Touching her breast.)* Here. I was in such pain, I could hardly breathe. I think he must have broken a rib. But he begged me not to go to Dr Morgan, he would guess how it had happened, and this is such a gossiping country–

MARY: Oh, poor Mama!

ELIZABETH: It still hurts. Tobacco is the only thing that eases the pain.

MARY: Oh, Mama –

She wants to embrace her, but ELIZABETH keeps her off.

ELIZABETH: I only break my promise to your Papa, so you can see how – He was generally a very kind man, but even the kindest men will sometimes do very unkind things in their passion for money. So – before you commit yourself to a husband, you must make sure not only that your fortune is safely secured to your own use, but that he fully understands that you will not give it up. People talk of money as an 'independence'. It is a good word. An independence secures genuine independence. Freedom, even, should you feel the need of it. Without it no woman in our sort of society can be truly happy. Which is what I want you to be.

MARY: *(Very touched.)* Thank you.

ELIZABETH: There! That is all the advice your mother has for you as you start your search for marital bliss!

They kiss. Then ELIZABETH goes, leaving MARY very thoughtful as PARRY comes on, carrying a paper.

MARY: *(To audience.)* And then summer came, no longer over the hills, but unavoidably here and now.

PARRY: *(To MARY.)* I've been making preparations for our marriage.

He sees her look.

We'll never have as fair an opportunity as now, with you in the country and your mama in Ross. *(Showing it.)* I've got a blank licence, look.

She is alarmed.

If you'll give me the ring with which we married each other in the sight of God, I'll go to Gloucester and have it copied and marked with our initials. A P in the middle for Parry and Powell, M for my darling Molly on one side and J for me on the other. That's all we'll need.

MARY: What about a parson?

PARRY: I asked Mr Jones to find us one and –

MARY: Which Mr Jones?

PARRY: My good friend at Dingestow.

MARY: *(Seizing on this.)* But he's a Roman Catholic! I'm not going to be married by a Roman catholic!

PARRY: You won't be. He's engaged the Anglican rector of Bryngwyn.

MARY: Davies! No, no! He's the greatest gossip on earth! He'll tell everyone from here to Hereford!

PARRY: *(Soothing.)* He won't. Because you will be wearing a mask, so he won't know who you are, and –

MARY: I'm not getting married in a mask.

PARRY: But he knows you. You'll have to.

MARY: Are you going to wear one too?

PARRY: No. He's never met me.

MARY: But our names – he'll have to know our names.

PARRY: They won't have to be revealed till the marriage is. Which won't be till you really do become with child.

MARY: *(To audience.)* Caught. In love – very much in love still – but wary, too, thinking of what my mother said. *(To PARRY.)* I'm sorry, Jemmy. I don't like it.

PARRY: Why not? What are you afraid of?

MARY: Matthew.

PARRY: No need for him to know anything about it.

MARY: He'll find out soon enough. The servants will tell him. And if they don't, half the people round here are his tenants, always spying on me, trying to get in his good books. And when he does find out – I've told you – he'll kill me.

PARRY: Of course he won't.

MARY: Or worse. *(Beat.)* He's – The feel of his hands on my body –

PARRY: He's evil, I agree, but –

MARY: *(Shudder.)* I wish he'd die!

PARRY: That would certainly solve everything. You would inherit Llantilio.

He stops, seeing her face.

I mean you would be free to do whatever you wish.

MARY: Would I?

She turns to the audience.

Jem rather let himself down there, didn't he? Showed himself to be not just a lover, but a player in the marriage market. I wondered, perhaps he had been all along. It's certainly what my mother would have thought. And if we were in the market – well! Ours is an old family, but our estate is small. We are comfortable, not rich, and certainly not fashionable. We do not go to London to attend court, or know which marquis is having an affair with which duchess. The nearest we get to that sort of life is the entertainment the Duke of Beaufort provides at the Monmouth races once a year for a few hundred people like ourselves, and that is tameness itself. We are ordinary country people, and live ordinary country lives. We have our disgraceful members, like my brother, but they do go to London, they don't scandalise us here. If and when I inherited I should continue to live here, where people would be horrified if I married a mere music master. They would refuse to receive me. And my mother would be mortified. *(Beat.)* Of course people can and do live in social isolation. But I did not wish to do so myself, and I certainly did not wish to impose isolation on Mama. So when he pressed our marriage in that forceful way, the less I wanted to go through with it. Though the music Jemmy and I made in bed was like all the cherubs of heaven singing together.

She gives him an inviting smile.

PARRY: *(Surprised.)* Now?

MARY: Why not?

PARRY: *(Delighted.)* You're insatiable!

MARY: Yes!

PARRY: Thank God!

They embrace passionately, then part.

MARY: The greater the danger, the greater pleasure. The Duchess of Malfi knew that, and so did I. It's easy to become too fond of heavenly music, and I had. Down here on earth, the flowers were again damnably delayed, so much so that this time I was certain I had a small cherub within me. *(Sombre.)* It was her children were the death of the poor Duchess. I didn't know what to do. I had no one to turn to, except Jemmy, and I knew he would make it another reason for our immediate marriage, and I wouldn't be able to argue. To have a legitimate life, the child had to be born in wedlock. Even if it meant my mother would never speak to me again. So I decided, against my own best judgement, I must marry him. Though I would give myself a few more days, hoping against hope – *(To PARRY.)* Where do you want the marriage to take place?

PARRY: Dingestow.

MARY: When?

PARRY: Saturday.

MARY: That's not possible. We have the beating of the parish bounds.

PARRY: Sunday, then.

MARY: All the farmers and tenants come to Great House on a Sunday. I have to be there to entertain them.

PARRY: Mary –

MARY: Make it Monday. I will come to Dingestow on Monday, I promise.

PARRY: Don't fail me.

MARY: I won't.

> *They kiss, then she goes. He starts to follow her, then turns back to address the audience, as he is joined by DAVIES, the parson.*

PARRY: *(To audience.)* On the Monday I put on my marriage suit – I was as foolish as Doomsday as to finery and had had it trimmed with silver. And I waited. And Mr Davies waited. We both waited. And waited. Until at last –

BETTY FISHER appears.

Betty? What's happened?

BETTY: Oh, sir, the most extraordinary thing – I could hardly believe it, if I hadn't seen it with my own two eyes –

PARRY: What, for God's sake?

BETTY: Well! There was a mad dog and bitch in the village, and somehow or other they got in among the Great House hounds! And they bit one or two of 'em real bad! So the huntsman and the gardener, they had to take the whole pack down the river this morning to where the tide comes up, to dip 'em all in salt water. It's the only thing for it, sea-water. And –

PARRY: But where's –

DAVIES takes a half-step forward to hear, which PARRY just sees in time.

Where's our friend?

BETTY: Oh, she's safe at home, sir, she didn't get bit.

PARRY: *(Beat.)* Then why isn't she here?

BETTY: There wasn't no one to ride over with her.

He looks at DAVIES, who shrugs.

She never rides out alone. It wouldn't be right.

PARRY: Not even to be married?

BETTY: She says to tell you she'll come tomorrow. Same time.

PARRY and DAVIES exchange another look. BETTY goes. PARRY gives DAVIES money.

PARRY: Tomorrow then?

DAVIES: And tomorrow. And, no doubt, tomorrow.

They start to go off, then turn and come back, as MARY appears.

MARY: *(To audience.)* On the Tuesday I could put it off no longer, and I set off to Dingestow with a very heavy heart. And then, suddenly, miraculously, as I jogged along, I felt the blessed flowers coming upon me. And I felt faint with joy because there was no need now to marry Jemmy Parry. And at the very same moment I knew for certain that I never would. I loved him still, but my life didn't have to be a tragedy, like that old play.

PARRY comes to greet her.

PARRY: Mary! At last!

He goes to kiss her, but she stops him.

MARY: I'm very sorry, James. I cannot marry you.

PARRY: Good God, what do you mean?

MARY: *(Very calm.)* If you do truly love and regard me, now is the time to show it. We can go on loving one another. It's simply that we cannot marry.

He begins to lose his temper.

PARRY: Cannot? After you have denied me the pleasures of
life these long years?

MARY: I thought rather I had granted them to you.

PARRY: God damn it! You would never let me go anywhere
I wanted – not to the music meetings at Hereford and
Worcester, where I might have improved myself by
discussing my profession with good masters. To speak to
any young woman – that was treason –

MARY: It was love. But I will never marry anyone without my
Mama's consent.

PARRY: The whole world knows I shall never have that.

She says nothing.

I have spent the flower of my youth in the rat-hole of Ross
to please you, when I could easily have gone to a better
place in a far more interesting town. Only you wouldn't
let me. You swore you would certainly marry me. Over
and over again. You said I wouldn't need to make music
my livelihood, for you had money enough for both of us.
Did you say that or not? *(Silence.)* You kept me here, solely
for your own diversion. And I stayed because I believed
that everything you said was sacred. *(Silence.)* Mary, for
heaven's sake, human happiness depends on our making
choices for ourselves. No one can be more proper than
yourself to decide who should be your husband. *(Trying
nobility.)* Look, here are all the love letters you've written
me since we first met.

He produces letters.

MARY: *(Apprehensive.)* Why have you brought these?

PARRY: Because they are full of your promises to marry
me, and I meant, once they were fulfilled, to burn them
as unfit for any eyes but our own. But now – since you
have treated me so abominably – faithlessly – you need
not imagine that your fortune shall screen you from my
resentment. Your letters are records that shall rise up in
judgement against you!

MARY: If you love me –

PARRY: If you loved me!

She bursts into tears.

Oh, tears, is it? The woman's first resort! Too late, Mary, too late. *(To audience.)* And yet, you know, even as I spoke to her so harshly, my heart was relenting, and I would, had it been in my power, have given millions to have her in my arms again.

He takes her hands.

(To MARY.) Farewell. I wish you all the happiness imaginable. And if you ever do marry, I shall earnestly pray that you may meet with a loving husband, who will make you happy.

She sobs.

And so you will have no reason to say I haven't behaved like a man of honour to the woman who has captivated him, I return these to you. *(Handing letters to her.)* Here. Do what you please with them. I bid you an eternal adieu.

She looks at the letters, then at him, then at the letters again. She strikes them from his hand and runs into his arms.

MARY: Don't go, don't go! You'll kill me!

PARRY: I have no choice.

MARY: Oh, God, your every word is a stab-wound!

PARRY: What do you want me to do? I have acted with as much honour as any man could towards you. I love you to distraction – but have been at great expense to no purpose. I don't mean money, I mean heart and soul. It's your person I covet, not your fortune. I've never wished more than to have you as my lawful wife. And I thought you never wished more, either. But no, so – farewell, happiness. Farewell, love.

She clings to him, making up her mind.

MARY: *(To audience.)* I wanted him. But not to marry. So I – prevaricated. *(To PARRY.)* I will marry you, Jemmy. In time. If you love me, you must give me time.

PARRY takes her in his arms.

PARRY: If! First shall the heavens bright lamp forget to shine,
    The stars shall from the azured sky decline;
    First shall the orient with the west shake hand,
    The centre of the world shall cease to stand,
    First wolves shall league with lambs, the dolphins fly,
    The Lawyer and physician fees deny;
    First heaven shall lie below and hell above,
    Ere I inconstant to my Mary prove.

MARY: *(To audience.)* He was always quoting.

She separates herself from him and he starts to pick up the letters she has dropped.

It was weak of me, I know. Dishonest. I was behaving like a man, not a woman. But if men treat love and marriage as two quite different things, why shouldn't we? Why are we called opprobrious names for doing that for which they are applauded? They don't marry their mistresses, why should we marry our lovers? We can and do still love them. But the woman in me was more sensible than the lover. She knew we had to stop the gossip. So she decided to ask my mother to come and stay with me at Llantilio. Great House was large, I thought Jemmy and I could always find ways to make love. Though, to tell the truth, it was never quite the same. The heart, you might say, had gone out of it. *(To PARRY, laughing but half-serious.)* You are not to keep company with lewd women while you're in Ross!

PARRY: *(To MARY.)* I know of no lewdness in Ross to compare with that of Llantilio!

Both laugh, but it is a wary, mature sort of laughter.

(To audience.) Madam Powell, damn her, once back there, never planned to move, so it was difficult to find times and places to consummate our passion. But we succeeded.

Music. She raises her skirt, he unbuttons his trousers, they get down to business; then hastily adjust their dress as ELIZABETH and BETTY FISHER come on and they go to play cards. We can see PARRY's foot pressing on MARY's; they exchange a quick smile. A trick is played. Then PARRY means to press MARY's foot again, but ELIZABETH suddenly cries out.

ELIZABETH: Oh, my corns!

PARRY: I'm so sorry, madam, I thought it was the table-leg.

MARY can scarcely stop herself laughing.

ELIZABETH: *(Cross.)* It's not funny, Mary.

MARY: No, Mama, Shall I get you a plaster?

ELIZABETH: Yes – no. I need to bathe them. Betty, will you come with me and –

BETTY: Of course, madam.

As ELIZABETH limps off with BETTY, MARY and PARRY are already preparing for sex and are soon interlocked again. They finish just in time before ELIZABETH limps back on again with BETTY.

ELIZABETH: My bid, I think.

PARRY: *(To audience.)* Bliss snatched is still bliss. And we found time and place enough until the sixth of October 1735. We were at the foot of the great staircase, when we thought everyone else was upstairs –

PARRY and MARY rush into one another's arms. He starts to unbutton, she raises her dress, and they are hard at it against the wall when PARRY suddenly pulls away.

Quick!

ELIZABETH is in time to see MARY disappearing and PARRY hauling his trousers up as fast as he can.

ELIZABETH: *(Incandescent.)* You cur, you dog, you – you Welsh thief! Leave this house!

PARRY: *(To audience.)* The white from the lime on the wall on the back of Mary's dress and the trousers round my ankles had betrayed us. Mrs Powell was no longer an indulgent mother but a sworn enemy. It was the last time Mary and I made love.

He stays and watches.

ELIZABETH: *(Calling.)* Mary! *(Sharper.)* Mary!

MARY appears, scared. ELIZABETH looks at her a long moment.

ELIZABETH: I have had a letter. You need not know from whom. It is about Mr Parry.

MARY: Oh?

ELIZABETH: It seems he has been boasting in a Ross ale-house that you would marry him, if he wished it. But he does not.

MARY is silent.

He said your face was damned ugly, your shape bad and your temper so stingy he could never endure it.

MARY gasps.

He also showed the company several letters he claimed you had written him.

MARY is appalled.

Have you written him letters?

MARY: *(No hesitation.)* Only about music.

ELIZABETH: There will be no more music. And you must never again be alone in his company.

MARY: Mama!

ELIZABETH: I cannot prevent your inheriting the Powell estate, if Matthew has no children. But I will not leave you a penny of my own money if you so much as think of James Parry again. I'd rather you married Dicky Jeffries!

She goes. MARY turns to the audience.

MARY: I was so narrowly watched, I scarcely had time to tie my garters. Mama made me share her bed in the hope I'd call out Jem's name in my sleep. I couldn't go on like that. But he kept returning to the gates of Great House, to the Ostrey inn, from where, though he could not get admission, he could at least communicate with me through the servants.

She watches as PARRY comes on, finishing a bottle of brandy. AMBROSE is with him, carrying another, which PARRY takes and starts on at once.

AMBROSE: *(Snigger.)* They do say, sir, as you've been teaching Miss the flute.

PARRY shakes his head without removing his lips from the bottle.

That is, the silent flute.

PARRY continues drinking.

The one that makes the invisible ink!

PARRY ignores him.

PARRY: *(To audience.)* I've been on my own in the world for most of my twenty-five years. I've had to fight for what I want. And if someone gives me a bloody nose, I'll give him a kick in the balls.

He finishes the bottle.

Another!

AMBROSE has it ready.

AMBROSE: They do say Miss is to marry Dicky Jeffries. He was mumbling and tumbling her in the churchyard last Sunday, and as he flung her down, forty people might have seen her arse. To say nothing of her –

PARRY: *(Sentimental drunk.)* Betty Brown, we called it. Betty Brown, with her regular inundations!

He starts on the new bottle.

MARY: *(To audience.)* If you're thinking, like the good sensible people you no doubt are, that no woman in my position should ever have let herself fall in love with a drunken wretch like this, then you are both right and wrong. Right that I should not have done so. And wrong because I was not then a woman, I was a girl, and you've forgotten the force and fury of first passion. *(She looks at him.)* Just as you can fall in love in an instant, so you can fall out again.

You look at your lover, and the life he leads you, and you remember how fine and handsome he was, how your blood seemed to speed through your veins every time you saw him. And you think of the many times you made love together, and how glorious it could be. But then you think – this man must never be the father of my children. I must stop it. It's stupid. So I wrote him a farewell letter. *(Beat, then to PARRY.)* I must now deal with you plainly. I cannot marry you. Now or ever.

PARRY staggers with a mixture of drink and surprise.

I therefore beg a last favour of you. That you will never think of me more. Nor write to me. I hope you will marry a more agreeable young woman than myself, and one with a greater fortune of her own. May all the happiness in this world and the next attend you. Goodbye.

PARRY stands there a moment, thunder-struck. Then he turns to the audience.

PARRY: Jilted! The perfidious whore! The damned false fiend! Jilted!

He stares round a moment, then picks up his whip and goes charging off as the lights change. Loud organ music.

In the darkness there is the sound of terrific hammering on a door.

(Off.) Mrs Powell! I want to speak to Mrs Powell!

BETTY: *(Off.)* She's not to be spoken with.

PARRY: *(Off.)* By God, I'll speak with her before I leave this place, or die on the spot!

BETTY: *(Off.)* She's not here, sir. Not at home.

PARRY: *(Off.)* Damn you, I know she is! Out of my way!

Sound of scuffle. BETTY screams.

MAN: *(Off.)* Come now, Mr Parry –

PARRY: *(Off.)* Out of my way, I said!

MAN: *(Off.)* You're forbidden the house!

PARRY reappears staggering backwards as if pushed.

PARRY: Hold, damn you – I have a wife here – a whore, anyway! I want to see her!

He flourishes his whip and charges back off again. More sounds of scuffle, screams, cursing, etc.

ELIZABETH: *(Off.)* Turn him out! Turn the rascal out!

PARRY is thrown back on stage again.

Lock the doors against him!

PARRY: *(Picking himself up, though staggering.)* Ah, the dulcet tones of the mother whore!

He charges off again. More hammering, scuffle, noise.

PARRY: *(Off.)* Let me in! I want to get an heir to the estate!

ELIZABETH: *(Off.)* Keep him out! Or we're all dead!

PARRY: *(Off.)* Out of my way!

Confusion, women screaming, men shouting. Then PARRY is thrown back on to the stage for the last time. He sits there a moment, stunned with drink and fighting. Organ fades. He shakes his head. He looks at the audience.

PARRY: Who are you looking at?

He gets to his feet, staggers.

A mug of ale! I said – a mug of ale!

He collapses again, unconscious.

MARY comes and looks at him.

MARY: *(To audience.)* I think he did love me, the way men love. But like all men he had an eye on his future comfort too.

She bends down, kisses PARRY on the top of his head.

Farewell, my ancient Briton.

He stirs, but by the time he opens his eyes, she has gone.

SEYS, a local magistrate, comes on with ELIZABETH. PARRY stirs, then sits up.

SEYS: He was so drunk he remembers nothing of what he did. When I told him, he said he was heartily sorry and would give you any satisfaction you require in the most public manner.

ELIZABETH: My satisfaction will be to see him transported. For forcible entry. He liked America when he was there before. He can see whether he likes it still.

SEYS: Madam –

ELIZABETH: I want revenge for Mary's honour.

SEYS: It will be flinging dirt in Miss Powell's face.

ELIZABETH: It is dirty already. Kindly take the affidavits of the servants who kept him out, and then commit him.

SEYS: He will get bail.

ELIZABETH: If anybody in this neighbourhood goes bail for him, I shall look upon them as my greatest enemy.

SEYS: I seriously advise you not to proceed with this. Parry can save, or ruin, your daughter's character irrevocably.

ELIZABETH: People may think what they like about my daughter – they will, anyway. But I would rather she were known as Parry's whore than his wife.

She goes, leaving SEYS unhappy. PARRY goes over to him.

PARRY: I thank you for your civility, Mr Seys. But there is a post going in Birmingham for an organist, and I'm told I stand a good chance of getting it. If Mrs Powell sends me to prison, and I lose the opportunity, I shall plague her and her family as long as they live.

SEYS: How will a mere music master do that?

PARRY: *(Angry.)* I'll publish her letters!

SEYS: *(Shocked.)* That would not be the act of a gentleman.

PARRY: I'm not a gentleman. Gentlemen are English, like you. They live in fine houses. They have servants. Their own accent. Their own code of manners. But I am a Welshman, and a musician. And I have my own code of revenge.

SEYS does not know what to say. But his curiosity gets the better of him.

SEYS: Is it true? I mean – Did you really – ?

PARRY: I have been in the carcass of her hundreds of times, if that's what you want to know. She has room there for a man's leg as well as his –

SEYS: *(Shocked.)* Parry!

PARRY: Do you think I was wrong to make love to a girl I loved?

SEYS: *(Judicial.)* No man can be criticised for trying to make his fortune, or for carrying on an intrigue – especially with a girl of Mary's age. If you have been upon her mount of Venus, and in the valley beneath it – well – . But after sweet meat comes sour sauce, and with Mrs Powell you will get it.

SEYS goes.

PARRY: *(Sings.)* Man may escape from rope and gun;
Nay, some have outlived the doctor's pill,
Who takes a woman must be undone,
That basilisk is sure to kill.
The fly that sips treacle is lost in the sweets;
So he that tastes woman ruin meets.

(Speech.) Captain Macheath was awaiting execution when he sang that, whereas I had only transportation to face. Which wouldn't have been so bad. They say there are communities in Pennsylvania where property is held in common, and marriage is truly a matter of love, not money. Or I could have found my way back to Carolina and Winifred Donning. For she hadn't drowned. That was a false report put about, I'm sure, to discourage me from returning and marrying her. No one has ever wanted me for their daughter, except the daughter herself.

DOOMSDAY comes on.

PARRY: Doomsday, my friend! Have you come to stand me bail?

DOOMSDAY: Certainly not! You have baulked me of a wife!

PARRY: By teaching her the art of love? You should be grateful. She has become an adept.

DOOMSDAY: A Balliol man cannot possibly marry the leavings of a mere music master!

PARRY: *(Fed up with him.)* You're a fool to think she would ever have had a man worth a 'mere' fifteen hundred pounds, when she'll be worth thousands. Balliol or no Balliol, you're too poor.

DOOMSDAY: By God, sir, if I were not a peaceable man – If I had no chance of marrying her, what made you imagine a poverty-stricken Welshman had one?

PARRY: Love. She loved me.

DOOMSDAY sneezes.

Physician, heal thyself! Have you decided yet when the world is coming to an end?

DOOMSDAY: Your world is ended now.

DOOMSDAY goes.

PARRY: He was right. But I still never thought of Mary without the utmost heart-breaking thoughts. We had parted so abruptly, I had so much still to tell her – I longed to see her one more time, to take a last farewell, if farewell it must be.

SEYS and MRS JEFFRIES come on with ELIZABETH, and a very reluctant MARY.

SEYS: He says he will give up Mary's letters, and go out of the country and never molest her more, if he may see her for five minutes alone.

It is as though MARY has not heard.

ELIZABETH: There are no such letters.

SEYS: Madam, I have seen them, they –

ELIZABETH: Forgeries. *(Furious and bitter.)* The scheming devious wretch would have starved in the streets if I had not invited him so often to dine. What he's eaten in my house for the last three years has stood me in two guineas a quarter. *(Recovering.)* Mary and I are going to Newport to charge him with forcible entry and assault.

MRS JEFFRIES: Good!

MARY: *(To audience.)* It was none of my doing. I had no desire for revenge. But I was no longer Mary Powell, I was Miss Powell of Llantilio again, a character in a play no longer my own. With no lines.

SEYS: Is this wise, Mary?

She says nothing. He sighs.

Very well.

He goes.

PARRY: *(To audience.)* And so – off I trudged to Newport! Where – I thought if we could just see each other again – I had loved her heart and soul, and she had loved me, and where love has flourished once – Perhaps the parting need not be final after all.

As the WOMEN start walking across the stage, PARRY stands where they must pass him. MARY's eyes are on the ground.

PARRY: *(With a great deal of ecstasy.)* How do you do, Mary?

She stops, sees him, and instantly looks away.

Won't you even look at me?

She will not.

It has been otherwise, Mary. Remember?

ELIZABETH: Move on, Mary!

She goes obediently on with ELIZABETH.

MRS JEFFRIES: *(Spiteful.)* Ha!

She follows. PARRY is left alone.

PARRY: She wouldn't even look at me. As though I wasn't there. That was the moment I decided I really would write up our affair. So she could never forget me, ever. Meanwhile –

Church bells ring out.

I was committed to Monmouth jail till the next sessions, and Mrs Powell ordered the church bells of Llantilio to ring all night and part of the next day to celebrate. But while the case dragged on for a year or more, sessions after sessions, with one whiffling charge following another, I wrote my book. *(Holds up book.)* Everyone was reading *Pamela* in those days. By Samuel Richardson. His heroine was a poor innocent virgin who withstands all the attacks of a man of fortune until he marries her. My case was the exact reverse. My heroine was a person of fortune who kept me for her pleasure, leading me on with thoughts of marriage, then jilting me. So I called this *The True Anti-Pamela*. It was finished at the same time as my case. *(Laugh.)* I was fined one shilling! Less than the price of a book which proved almost as popular as its model.

MRS JEFFRIES comes on reading it.

MRS JEFFRIES: *(Eagerly turning pages.)* Shocking!

DOOMSDAY comes on the other side, also reading.

DOOMSDAY: A pimple? Why didn't she come to me? I'm the doctor!

ELIZABETH comes on, very grim, also reading.

ELIZABETH: *(Furious.)* The cur! The filthy cur!

MRS JEFFRIES: *(Lip-licking.)* Disgusting!

DOOMSDAY: I could have told her dittany was no good.

ELIZABETH: Ungrateful wretch!

MRS JEFFRIES: Disgraceful!

DOOMSDAY: Betty Brown? What does that – Oh!

ELIZABETH: Welshman!

As they all go off, still reading, MARY comes on, carrying the book.

PARRY: It was specially successful in Ross and Monmouth. People frowned and shook their heads, even as they read my every word.

MARY: Some people will always enjoy a public execution.

PARRY: Execution? But I've made you famous to all posterity!

She just looks at him. He realises he has gone too far.

Oh, I'm sure all these good people are shaking their heads and saying what a heartless rogue and blackguard I am. *(Mock sorrow.)* I heartily wish I could have omitted the more *private* circumstances of our amour – glad, for my own sake as much as yours, to forget them altogether. But so many people came to receive such inaccurate reports of it I felt I owed it to them – and you – to tell the whole truth. I, therefore, though with a heavy heart, left nothing out.

MARY: I suppose the publisher made you put that in.

PARRY: *(Slightly ashamed.)* Well – But you ruined me. I spent the best part of my youth, and the quintessence of my blood, to satisfy your lust. And then – Do you think Birmingham or anywhere else would have me after what you swore against me?

MARY: It was my mother's decision to prosecute, not mine.

PARRY: The idea that women are weak! Women with money. You'd inherited your brother's estate, and you had your mother's to come. I was penniless.

MARY: You had enough money to buy liquor. We heard of you brawling in the streets of London.

PARRY: It was a matter of honour.

MARY: If you knew anything of honour – When a woman is exposed like that – It was like being tied naked to the back of a cart and whipped through the streets, while people jeered and threw eggs and vegetables and filth, sometimes stones, while others emptied chamber-pots on me from upstairs windows. Are you pleased that's what you did to me? *(Beat.)* Why did you do it?

PARRY: *(Pious, reading.)* 'After all that had happened, my nearest relations would not look upon me until I justified myself to the world'.

MARY: The publisher made you put that in too, I suppose.

PARRY shrugs.

You were always hiding your true feelings behind other men's words. But your book hasn't even had the result you intended. You meant to present yourself as my victim. But most readers will think that I was yours. *(To audience.)* Don't you? *(To PARRY.)* Why did you write it? Truthfully?

PARRY: *(Bursting out.)* Because I honestly believed no passion had ever equalled ours, and – and you destroyed it. *(Beat.)* Why wouldn't you marry me? *(Silence.)* Was it because I am Welsh?

MARY: I have nothing against the Welsh. In fact I married a Welshman. From Carmarthen.

PARRY: Oh yes! One of the lawyers who persecuted me! A man with two estates already! That's how the rich get ever richer, breeding together. *(He regrets this at once; beat.)* Was he as much in love with you as I was?

MARY: *(Beat.)* He made a much better husband.

PARRY: And were you as much in love with him as you were with me?

MARY: *(Sigh.)* No. But – I had my children.

PARRY: We could have had children. Love children.

MARY: *(Another sigh.)* No.

PARRY: *(Beat.)* My soul is so strongly divided. Your perfidiousness makes me hate you. Yet my love obstinately remains. I cannot think of anyone else but you.

MARY: Perhaps you should have taken your cousin's advice and had the operation.

PARRY: And missed the greatest joy of my life? My book testifies to that, you must admit. If it ends in great hate, it begins with great love.

MARY: Was it love?

PARRY: *(To audience.)* What do you think? *(Laugh.)* Doomsday was wrong, as you may have noticed. The world has not ended, though it has for us. Mary has a marble memorial in the church at Llantilio. I – I was shot in the Canary Islands, raiding with a privateer. They buried me at sea. But my book lives on. So we do, too.

MARY: Dead, but unable to die.

PARRY: Like our love.

MARY: If it was love.

PARRY: Oh, it was, it was!

MARY: *(Sigh.)* Yes. But you wanted marriage as well. And love and marriage are two such very different things.

PARRY: Then you did love me?

MARY: Oh, yes. *(To audience.)* Don't you think?

They begin to sing 'Over the Hills and Far Away'. *As they come to the final chorus they begin to go off on opposite sides, not looking at each other. They disappear, still singing. As the song ends, slow fade to black.*

OTHER JULIAN MITCHELL TITLES

FAMILY BUSINESS
9781849430951

THE GOOD SOLDIER
By Ford Madox Ford, Adapted by Julian Mitchell
9781849430203

WWW.OBERONBOOKS.COM

 Follow us on www.twitter.com/@oberonbooks
& www.facebook.com/oberonbook

www.ingramcontent.com/pod-product-compliance
Ingram Content Group UK Ltd.
Pitfield, Milton Keynes, MK11 3LW, UK
UKHW020724280225
455688UK00012B/499